Praise for

DAILY
DEVOTIONAL

"These reflections are clear, compelling,
lovely, and warmly inviting."

Steve McCarthy
Executive Director, United Way St. Croix and Red Cedar Valleys

"His first book, *SuperHuman Being*, proved he could
write with heart and insight; this one takes that wisdom
straight into the everyday practice of recovery."

Abby Medcalf, PhD
Therapist, Author, and Podcaster

"I look forward each day to reading what Larry
shares. He has a way with words, a true gift."

Elizabeth Bartz
Behavior Health Training Partnership
CW-Green Bay, Wisconsin

"He writes with careful, honest, and authentic words from his
heart. His career in social work and personal life experiences
provides a unique and knowledgeable perspective. What
I like best is that the reflections stirs my curiosity to learn
more about myself, educates, and provides hope in the
personal journeys we all are on despite our differences."

Julie

"The daily messages are a port in the storm."

Suz

"L. J. Winter's ability to capture the exact message that supports
persons in recovery is phenomenal! It is the perfect mixture of
'I have walked the journey of hard experiences' and the tools
and hope needed to move forward in the recovery journey."

Paula

DAILY
DEVOTIONAL

12 STEPS to Unshakeable Recovery

L.J. WINTER

ISBN 979-8-9870127-3-4 (ebook)
ISBN 979-8-9870127-4-1 (paperback KDP)
ISBN 979-8-9870127-5-8 (paperback LSI)

SELO 43000 SELF-HELP/Recovery
SELO 29000 SELF-HELP/Twelve Step
PSY 036000 PSYCHOLOGY/ Mental Health

Cover design and typesetting by Kaitlin Barwick

superhumanbeing.net

To my three beautiful daughters,
McKenzie, Katrina, and Lexi.
Watching you grow into beautiful and
wise women makes me a proud dad.

ABOUT THE COVER

Why is the cover the color green, and what does the ribbon represent?

Across the United States, nearly one in five adults live with a mental health condition. Still, stigma remains one of the largest barriers to adults seeking help. The Green Bandana Project began on university campuses and is now expanding to communities across the United States. For more information and to get your own Bandana, go to The Bandana Project: thebandanaproj.org/contact

Supporting and wearing a Green Bandana will help change the conversation by reducing stigma affiliated with mental health, substance misuse, and trauma. It opens a conversation about mental health experiences.

Wearing the bandana or attaching it to a purse or backpack in public indicates that you are

- a safe person to approach with a mental health–related issue.
- willing to listen.
- knowledgeable about the resources available in your area.
- able to provide help and support in times of crisis.

FOREWORD

by Abby Medcalf, PhD

I've been going to Twelve Step meetings since 1983, which means I know two things for sure: the coffee at meetings is always either too strong or too weak, and trying to live the steps outside the meeting room can feel like assembling IKEA furniture without the little Allen wrench.

That's why Larry Winter's new book is such a gift. I met Larry in our author's mastermind years ago, and his mix of grounded wisdom and unforced kindness reminds me of the best people I've met in recovery rooms. He's the real deal—steady, thoughtful, and deeply committed to helping people heal without ever taking himself too seriously.

His first book, *SuperHuman Being*, proved he could write with heart and insight; this one takes that wisdom straight into the everyday practice of recovery.

Daily Devotional is exactly what so many of us have wished for: a day-by-day instruction manual for living the steps when real life barges in. Each reflection is short enough to read while you're waiting for the microwave to ding but sturdy enough to stick with you when the day gets loud. They nudge you to practice mindfulness when your mind is sprinting, to face facts when denial feels easier, and to remember that imperfection isn't failure, it's the point.

Whether you're new to the program or have a few decades under your belt, you'll find something here that makes the steps feel alive, not just words on a wall. Larry shows you how to live Recovery in traffic, at work, in the kitchen, and in all the messy in-between moments where it really counts.

Crack the spine, pick today's page, and let these reflections guide you. They won't do the work for you, but they'll keep you company while you do the work that matters.

Don't leave before the miracle,

Abby Medcalf, PhD

Psychologist, Author, and Person in Long-Term Recovery

INTRODUCTION

I have been in Recovery for thirty years. During this time, I have used several 365-day daily devotionals to strengthen my emotional, mental, and spiritual health. This book is written with the hope that it will be an inspirational companion to my first book, *SuperHuman Being: Be Bold, Be Imperfect, Be Present, and Recover.* However, these daily reflections stand alone without having to read my original work.

These gentle reflections also offer concrete actions to guide our Recovery. Next to each day, there is a number that connects to one of the Twelve Steps to Mental Wellness. A full copy of my adaptation of the Twelve Steps is included at the end of this book. The term *God* also means *Higher Power.* These steps work for anyone—whether we call on the Christian God or another spiritual Higher Power.

The original Twelve Steps were created in 1935 by Bill Wilson and Dr. Robert Smith, the cofounders of Alcoholics Anonymous (AA). They drew wisdom from the Oxford Group and shaped the steps to help people recover from alcoholism. Over the years, these steps have been adapted by many groups to meet different needs. In this book, the steps are offered especially for people facing mental health struggles and substance misuse.

I hope this book will be our conversation with Recovery itself. Life often brings us moments of anxiety, sadness, anger, or being overwhelmed. Isn't it comforting to know we are not alone? Some days these reflections may lead us into gratitude. Other days, they may guide us toward forgiveness for harm we have caused or remind us of our need for help. Many of us find peace through a relationship with God, our Higher Power. Several reflections invite us to rest in the compassion of our Father, who loves us deeply. If we open our hearts, we may even hear His voice between the lines.

We can use this book in many different ways:

- Start with the first day and move forward.
- Flip through the pages until we find a topic that speaks to our need.
- Read together in a support group, offering encouragement to one another.
- Keep a journal of our thoughts and how we will practice each reflection.

There is no single "right way" to approach Recovery. The reading and application of these words are meant to be personal and flexible, meeting us where we are on our journey of hope, healing, and health.

DAY 1

Awaken to the Now

Mindfulness invites us to embrace the present moment with open hearts. It helps us let go of thoughts that drain us and brings us back to what is real and sacred: *this moment*. When we live with awareness, we become participants in our healing, not just observers.

Sit or lie down comfortably. Close your eyes and focus on your breath. After two minutes, gently notice your surroundings. What do you hear, see, feel? Stay present for five to ten minutes. End by returning focus inward to your breath. When you're ready, open your eyes—awake, grounded, and renewed.

DAY 2

The Gift of Imperfection

Our humanity makes us imperfect. It is in embracing these imperfections that we find freedom. Accepting ourselves allows us to try new things, face the unknown without fear, and show compassion when we stumble. True growth and healing emerge when we release the need to be flawless. Our perfection lies not in faultlessness but in the courage to be human.

DAY 3

STEP #7

The Gift of a Wise Mind

In Recovery, both our reasonable mind and emotional mind are at work. Reason offers facts and logic; emotion brings passion and feeling. Alone, each can mislead us. Together, they create a *wise mind*, like instruments blending in harmony.

A wise mind listens to both truth and feeling, guiding us toward balance. Even in life's storms, it offers a safe place of peace and clarity. This skill takes practice, patience, and trust. By centering ourselves in our wise mind, we learn to respond, not react, and find freedom to take the next right step.

DAY 4

STEP #10

The River of Self-Awareness

Self-awareness connects us to our mind, heart, and soul, engaging our senses and inner dialogue. At times, we may cover it up to avoid uncomfortable thoughts and feelings. But deep self-awareness is the bridge to lifelong Recovery.

True self-awareness moves us from dipping a toe into the river to fully diving in. By observing our thoughts and sensations, subtle or intense, we learn, adjust, and grow. When we swim with this current, we flow toward healing and deeper Recovery.

Embrace practices and moments that nurture your self-awareness and allow curiosity and courage to guide you along the path of transformation.

DAY 5

Taming the Inner Snowstorm

Recovery is hard, yet possible. Even amidst the snowstorm of swirling emotions, self-awareness helps us understand the impact of our inner dialogue. By observing our thoughts and feelings with curiosity, we can let go of those that do not support our healing.

Thoughts and feelings are like snowflakes: some melt away unnoticed while others we taste and savor. Naming them, speaking them aloud, or recording them gives us the power to transform our inner weather. With patience and gentle attention, we learn to manage the storm and find clarity, peace, and growth on our Recovery journey.

DAY 6

The Gift of Mindfulness

Mindfulness is living fully in the present, calmly acknowledging and accepting our thoughts, feelings, and bodily sensations. Practicing mindfulness balances our joys and sorrows, strengthening our capacity to heal mentally, emotionally, spiritually, and physically.

Sit or lie comfortably, eyes open or closed, and focus on your breath. When a thought or feeling arises, notice it, then let it go. Practice for five minutes or longer, daily if possible.

Mindfulness moves us from past burdens into the present, where the quiet whispers of our hearts guide us toward clarity, hope, and the gentle pursuit of our dreams.

DAY 7

Floating Thoughts

Mindfulness invites us to listen to the voice within without judgment.

By practicing nonjudgment, we connect with our creative self, learning to see thoughts without labeling them as good or bad, right or wrong. Curiosity softens their grip, freeing our hearts.

Take a judgmental thought and mentally place it on a leaf. Imagine setting the leaf afloat on a river. As it drifts away, the thought releases its hold, allowing you to be fully present, open, and free to create in the quiet, unfolding moment of now.

DAY 8

The Power of Presence

Scattered thoughts can hijack our minds, but mindfulness frees us to engage fully in life. Our minds are designed to focus on one task at a time. When we drift or escape into fantasies, we miss the solutions Recovery offers.

Consider an apple tree. It does one thing: produce apples. By feeding its roots with water, it grows strong and bears fruit. Likewise, when we focus on the present moment, nurturing our hearts and minds, we cultivate clarity, strength, and the ability to thrive in Recovery.

DAY 9

The Power of Facts

In Recovery, focusing on facts fosters constructive action. Acting solely on emotions can harm ourselves and others. Ignoring challenges only allows them to persist.

By grounding ourselves in facts and approaching others with patience and love, we create understanding, connection, and healing, both for ourselves and for those we connect with on our Recovery journey.

When interacting with others, seek truth with fairness and compassion. Gently assert yourself while remaining open to their perspective. Relax your mind and listen deeply, showing respect and honoring their voice.

DAY 10

STEP #3

Weathering the Storm

Distressing emotions can feel overwhelming, even leading to a mental health crisis. Distress tolerance helps us withstand floods of feelings, resisting urges to isolate, misuse substances, act violently, or think destructively.

By accepting our emotions without judgment, our darker tendencies gradually wash away. Shadows give way to a clear sky, bringing peace and calm into our lives.

These difficult emotions stretch our capacity for patience and resilience. There is no need to feed destructive impulses. Simply observing and allowing them to pass nurtures healing, strength, and inner tranquility on our Recovery journey.

DAY 11

Inviting the Wise Mind

Life's circumstances can stir strong feelings that block our ability to cope. Yet we are not powerless. There are ways to regulate our urges.

- A few deep breaths can soften intensity.
- Taking a break allows space for clarity.
- Checking in with our senses (what we see, think, and feel in our body) grounds us in the present.

When we pause and create space within, the mind and heart gently step forward to address the issue with both emotion and reason. From this place of balance, healing and peace become possible.

DAY 12

STEP #1

Finding Calm in the Storm

A rainstorm may cause a boat to capsize, just as emotional flooding can make us feel like we are drowning. Between the chaos and the calm, suffering often arises. Yet even in the eye of the storm, we can choose to remain grounded and move toward safety. And sometimes, the very storms we fear become the waters that carry us closer to healing.

Think back to a time of suffering in your life. Beyond the current struggle, what lessons, gifts, or relationships grew from that experience to help in future barriers standing in the way? What meaning did it hold?

DAY 13

Calm for the Soul

We can ease our burdens by opening ourselves to prayer and relaxation. Much like Jesus calming the sea, prayer invites us to set aside distractions, surrender control to God (or our Higher Power), and find peace within. Though prayer may not remove suffering, it soothes the soul.

Relaxation also restores balance, whether through a warm bath, deep breathing, yoga, or simple stillness. When mind and body are calm, we are better able to manage the weight of mental health, trauma, and Recovery.

DAY 14

Calm in the Cyclone

When an emotional cyclone shakes our mind, body, and soul to the core of our being, we can choose gentle ways to restore balance. Focusing on one task at a time unites us within. A brief "vacation" can refresh our minds and bodies, even something as simple as turning off the phone, resting on a blanket in the park, or watching a movie.

We can also heal through prayer, meditation, relaxation, imagery, or simple mindfulness. Each practice gives our soul space to breathe. Which of these might guide you today toward peace and healing?

DAY 15

Sharing Hope in Recovery

Recovery calls us to serve one another with compassion. We can be a joyful witness to our brothers and sisters on this journey. Can you recall a time when you offered hope to someone in need? People are looking to us; we need to be who we say we are.

When we share our story, we remind others that healing is possible. Though our paths may differ, together we walk on equal ground, offering hope, love, and joy.

DAY 16

Hope Protects Our Joy

In Recovery, we may long for hope and joy, especially in times of suffering. Trusting the process allows both to gently appear. Hope will keep us from despair, and it will protect the joy in our lives.

At day's end, self-reflection helps us see that recovery is not only about healing but also about experiencing joy.

DAY 17

Choosing with Wisdom

Making decisions can stir anxiety. When emotions run high, step back and allow the intensity to ease. Then invite your wise mind to help.

Use a pros-and-cons list to see clearly. What are the positive outcomes of thoughtful choices? What harm may come if emotions lead the way?

When you are tempted to say, "I'm tired of recovery," write the pros and cons of stopping. Consider the consequences of each choice, then prayerfully select the path that brings you hope and peace.

DAY 18

Embracing Radical Acceptance

Radical Acceptance means fully embracing reality—our emotions, struggles, and circumstances—without denial or resistance. It allows us to surrender bitterness and cope with suffering, anger, and pain.

Life is messy and complicated, yet joy can still take root. Nurture it daily. Seek hope in those who listen, believe your story, and walk with you on recovery's bumpy road. In acceptance, peace begins.

DAY 19

The Peace of Radical Acceptance

Radical Acceptance means embracing reality, even when it's not what we hoped for. To do this, we seek the truth and face the facts, even the hard ones.

Life is still beautiful and worth living, even with pain. *It is what it is* because we share this world with imperfect human beings, like ourselves. When we choose Radical Acceptance, peace begins to grow in our hearts.

DAY 20

The Hope Within Acceptance

Why practice Radical Acceptance? Because rejecting reality doesn't change it; it deepens our suffering. Pain is often a signal that something needs attention, but denial traps us in anger, anxiety, or shame.

Acceptance may feel dark at first, yet within that darkness, a flicker of hope remains. By embracing our emotions and circumstances, we allow light to return, little by little, until peace fills our hearts again.

DAY 21

STEP #11

Turning the Mind Toward Hope

Radical Acceptance doesn't mean suffering will never return, but it gives us tools to cope. When thoughts say, *Why me?* or *It shouldn't be this way*, we can choose to turn our mind in a new direction, like stepping off a merry-go-round that keeps us stuck.

Explore new paths with prayer, reflection, and even a simple pros-and-cons list. Manage distress, create a plan, and take action. True strength is born not from following what feels easy but from overcoming what once felt impossible.

DAY 22

The Beauty of Willingness

Radical Acceptance invites us to live fully by practicing willingness—doing what's needed without delay. Like a turtle crossing the road, hesitation can be dangerous.

Willingness means listening to our wise mind, balancing logic and emotion, and taking bold action. It's trusting the inner voice that says, *We've got this*, even when the path feels uncertain. In willingness, we discover the mystery and beauty of being fully alive.

DAY 23

STEP #1

Choosing Willingness Over Willfulness

Willfulness resists reality; it refuses change, clings to control, and blocks healing. Willingness, however, opens the door to life by fully participating in the present.

When willfulness rises, notice it. Radically accept its presence instead of fighting it. By owning our story and loving ourselves through these moments, we discover courage. These small acts become some of the bravest steps we will ever take on our Recovery journey.

DAY 24

STEP #3

Opening to Peace

Healing begins when we open to the present, accept reality, and invite calm.

In times of stress, try a half-smile: Relax your face, gently lift the corners of your lips, and let tension soften.

Practice willing hands: Stand, drop your arms, and open your palms outward and upward, fingers relaxed.

Your body speaks to your mind, reminding you that peace is possible. The mind can be your strongest ally or greatest enemy. Train it with gentle awareness, and rediscover the self God created you to be.

DAY 25

Finding Balance in Distress

A clear mind is a wise mind, valuing both reason and emotion. But how do we find balance when distress takes over? By gently redirecting our attention. This isn't ignoring pain; it's creating space to breathe.

Even simple moments of healthy distraction can help regulate emotions, giving us clarity to return to our challenges with strength and peace.

When you find yourself giving into distress, choose one of these simple actions to help recenter and calm your mind before returning to face the challenge: complete a task, watch a movie, attend an event, play a sport, share a meal, build something, or do a puzzle.

DAY 26

STEP #12

The Gift of Contributing

Helping others nurtures our own emotional health and brings balance to our minds, even simple acts like volunteering, helping a friend, sending an encouraging message, decluttering and donating, creating something special, or surprising someone with kindness.

These moments deepen our connections and invite our wise mind to guide us through challenges. When we contribute to others, we not only lift their spirits but also help them become the best version of themselves. And in doing so, we grow too.

DAY 27

STEP #1

Finding Perspective Through Comparison

Healthy comparison can bring balance when life feels heavy.

Comparison isn't about feeling superior. It's about recognizing growth and strength. By seeing how far we've come, we lessen emotional pain and regain clarity. Sometimes, a shift in perspective is the first step toward peace.

Reflect on times you've faced challenges before, or notice others coping with similar or greater struggles. Watch stories on television of resilience or simply refocus by helping someone else.

DAY 28

Shifting Emotions with Purpose

When distress triggers strong urges, short-term distractions can help us regulate emotions. Try reading an emotional story, watching a heartfelt movie, listening to music, browsing old photos, or attending a sporting event to observe the energy of others.

Choose activities that stir a different feeling from the one troubling you. This shift can lighten the burden and bring relief. Remember: emotions come and go. With patience and hope, we can move through any moment and find peace again.

DAY 29

The Gentle Art of Pushing Away

Pushing away is a tender coping strategy, a way to step back from difficult thoughts or situations until we're ready to face them with strength. This can be as simple as taking a break: leave the room, do a puzzle, or engage in a brief distraction.

The key is not avoidance, but when our mood is tamed, we return gently and intentionally, and we approach challenges with clarity, compassion, and renewed peace.

Create a worry box: When feeling overwhelmed, place your thoughts inside a mental (or physical) box and return to them when you are calm. How is your approach to the challenge different from if you had reacted emotionally in the moment?

DAY 30

Redirecting the Mind for Peace

During distress, gentle distraction allows us to shift attention and invite our wise mind to guide us. Simple practices (counting to ten, noticing colors in a painting, repeating a song, doing puzzles, reading, or recalling joyful memories) can ease emotional intensity.

Our thoughts can either lift us toward wellness or pull us into darkness. By turning inward and connecting with something greater than ourselves, we create calm and clarity, finding balance even amid difficult emotions.

DAY 31

Sensing Peace in the Moment

When emotions or urges feel overwhelming, turning to our senses can help us cope. Try squeezing a stress ball, listening to music, holding an ice bag on your face, stepping into the rain or snow, taking a hot or cold shower, gazing at the stars, savoring a dessert, or engaging in physical activity.

Using our senses grounds us, offering calm in vulnerable moments. These simple practices help us navigate challenges, bringing presence, clarity, and gentle relief to difficult emotions or urges.

DAY 32

STEP #8

Nurturing Meaningful Connections

Interpersonal relationships are a gift, yet they can be challenging when unresolved trauma, mental health struggles, or unhealthy behaviors remain.

Healthy relationships grow through mindful communication: ask for help, share opinions, calmly say no, avoid people-pleasing, and prioritize healing.

Our desire for connection is woven into our mind, heart, and soul. We are worthy of being heard and understood. By honoring our deepest needs and acting with wisdom, we cultivate meaningful bonds and find our place in the world.

DAY 33

Cultivating Healthy Relationships

Relationships are like gardens: daily care nurtures growth, while neglect allows weeds to take over.

We may need to let go when boundaries are violated, trust is broken, accountability is absent, or mutual care is missing. Healthy relationships offer honesty, safety, and generosity.

In Recovery, recognizing someone is no longer supportive can bring grief. That's natural. Our priority is honoring our healing and growth, creating space for relationships that nurture our heart, mind, and soul.

DAY 34

The Gift of Relationships

Relationships are about giving and receiving, meeting our needs while honoring the other's strengths. Sometimes, we may need to end destructive connections.

Consider two friends: intelligent, hardworking, and alike in many ways. Could they support each other for a lifetime?

Relationships are spiritual gifts meant to nurture care, compassion, and fulfillment. By serving, loving, and supporting one another, we experience true fellowship.

DAY 35

Nurturing Healing Through Connection

Cultivating connection with others is essential to Recovery. Experiences and perception beyond our own circle provides space to heal and grow.

Approach interactions with respect and kindness, even during challenges. Avoid verbal or physical attacks, blame, judgment, or dismissive behavior. Speak calmly, without sneering, eye-rolling, or minimizing feelings.

Gentle, compassionate communication builds trust, understanding, and closeness. Take a moment to reflect on how speaking with care can strengthen relationships, support mutual healing, and nurture both our growth and the well-being of those around us.

DAY 36

The Gift of Genuine Interest

When we truly listen to another, we honor their worth. Facing them, holding eye contact, leaning in with openness—these simple acts say, *your voice matters.* Listening without interruption and seeking a kernel of truth in their words requires humility and maturity.

Research shows connection is expressed through body language (55%), tone (38%), and words (7%). By being present, we communicate far more than speech alone. Genuine interest validates another's thoughts and feelings, creating a safe space where understanding can flow both ways, first to understand, and then to be understood.

DAY 37

The Grace of an Easy Manner

We are often drawn to those who bring lightness—a smile, a gentle word, a touch of humor. We, too, can embody this spirit. When using humor, let it be at our own expense, never another's, and keep sarcasm aside.

A gentleness shines through kindness, warmth, and openness. It means softening our approach, setting ego aside, and allowing others to feel safe in our presence. In return, we may discover hidden rewards: spontaneity, intimacy, and generosity. With gentleness, relationships become mutual blessings where we can say with gratitude, "I have received as much as I have given."

DAY 38

Gentle Strength in Relationships

Relationships are often complex, and even small misunderstandings can spark conflict. Yet, with care, we can turn tense moments into opportunities for peace. The practice of **DEARMAN** offers a gentle guide: *Describe* the situation, *Express* your feelings, *Assert* your needs, *Reinforce* your position, stay *Mindful*, *Appear* confident, and *Negotiate* when needed.

The goal is not to win an argument but to stay rooted in truth and compassion. By speaking with honesty, staying grounded in facts, and responding with gentleness, we nurture respect, preserve connection, and strengthen the bond of understanding.

DAY 39

The Courage to Be Real

When we gently express our feelings, we affirm our worth and honor our true self. Using "I" statements (such as "I feel anxious when plans change" or "I feel sad when you arrive late") helps us take responsibility without placing blame. Phrases like "I feel guilty" rather than "You make me feel guilty" create space for honesty and compassion.

By calmly naming our emotions, we invite understanding, increase the chance of having our needs met, and open the door to deeper, more authentic connections.

DAY 40

STEP #5

The Gift of Healthy Boundaries

Recovery teaches us to balance caring for others with honoring our own needs. At times, we may fear that asserting ourselves is selfish, yet the facts often reveal otherwise. Assertiveness is not aggression; it is calm strength that recognizes dignity, sets boundaries, and invites respect.

Simple statements like "Please ask before entering my office" or "I've already said no; please don't ask again" affirm our worth. By asserting ourselves with gentleness, we care for our needs while showing love and respect to others.

DAY 41

The Boldness of Boundaries

In relationships, asking for what we need requires both courage and patience. When our "no" is ignored, it becomes a moment to gently but firmly reinforce our boundary. At times, persistence may call for responses like "Let's stop talking about this now" or "I'm not going to change my mind."

Rejection may come, yet each time we stand by our boundaries, we grow in confidence. By expressing ourselves with calm strength, we release past fears and step into healthier, more authentic connections.

DAY 42

Honoring Our Needs with Mindfulness

Becoming mindful of our wants and needs in relationships takes trust, patience, and courage. It means moving away from "shoulds" and choosing self-care instead. When we notice our inner dialogue, we're less likely to let fear or feelings silence us. Often, we ignore our needs because we fear rejection.

Practicing mindfulness helps us pause, accept our experiences (pleasant or not), and respond with honesty. The alternative is sacrificing who we are, which only benefits others at our expense. Choosing mindfulness affirms both our worth and our voice.

DAY 43

STEP #3

Practicing Confidence

Before we feel confident, we can practice looking confident. Rehearse what you want to say, use a steady voice, keep a calm posture, and make eye contact. Avoid stammering, whispering, or shrinking away. Phrases like "This is important to me" or "I believe this approach will work" can strengthen your message.

Appearing confident often leads to genuine confidence. It signals that our needs matter and deserve to be heard. Even if we don't get what we want, staying true to ourselves empowers us to walk away with peace and self-respect.

DAY 44

Negotiating with Respect and Integrity

Meeting our wants and needs often requires negotiation, a willingness to give and seek solutions. When a request conflicts with our values or boundaries, it's okay to say no, then offer an alternative that feels right for both.

For example, propose a solution like:

"How about you call if you'll be late?"

Or "I can't do that, but what do you think I should do?"

Negotiation empowers us to stay true to ourselves while honoring others. It's about creating balance, not sacrificing who we are to keep the peace.

DAY 45

STEP #8

Questions That Build Healthy Relationships

Before entering a relationship, it helps to ask yourself a series of questions:

- *Am I an effective communicator?*
- *What do I need from this relationship?*
- *How will I know if it fosters my growth?*
- *What will I do if it does not feed my heart?*

These questions may seem unsettling, but finding answers ahead of time brings peace and confidence. Recovery reminds us we are worthy of relationships that support our well-being . . . and strong enough to walk away when they do not. Asking these questions is an act of self-respect and hope for something beautiful.

DAY 46

Holding Self-Respect in Relationships

Maintaining self-respect in relationships is a sign of growth in Recovery. Ask yourself: *What throws me off track when interacting with someone? What helps me return to balance?*

Be fair, to them and to yourself, especially in tense moments. Validate their feelings without losing your voice. Avoid over-apologizing or shrinking back; never apologize for having an opinion or disagreeing respectfully.

When we advocate for our needs with calm strength, we nurture love, purpose, and respect for ourselves and create space for healthier, more meaningful connections.

DAY 47

The Freedom of Living Truthfully

Sticking to our values and speaking truth deepens our self-respect. As John wrote, *"The truth shall set you free"* (John 8:32).

In relationships, don't ignore your values. Clarity about what we believe reflects our moral compass. Truthful conversations help resolve issues and honor both needs. Avoid acting helpless, exaggerating, or making excuses; simply state the facts.

When we live in truth, our inner safety grows. We trust ourselves, the war within ends, and freedom begins. We become who we were created to be: whole, authentic, and at peace.

DAY 48

The Power of Healthy Boundaries

Recovery embraces opposites: we can be strong and gentle, desire solitude yet seek connection, share openly while keeping some things private, or disagree and remain friends.

Through self-awareness and establishing boundaries, we notice how these contrasts influence both ourselves and others. Seeing another's perspective can shift our thinking when the facts support it.

Practicing this approach can ease sadness, anger, reduce anxiety, and curb urges to misuse substances. Even when situations remain unchanged, our spiritual growth deepens, revealing clarity, healing, and a fuller sense of peace.

DAY 49

The Joy of Surrender

Healing draws us closer to God. Recovery is ongoing; it doesn't end when therapy or a support group session ends. Those moments prepare us to live differently in the everyday.

When our hearts are open, it is easy to surrender to our Higher Power: *"Lord, Your will be done"* (Matthew 6:10). In that surrender, we find freedom and strength. Recovery is about trusting God and living His way. When we let go and allow Him to lead us, peace returns to our lives.

DAY 50

Changing Our Inner Weather

Recovery is possible even when storms rage within us. Our inner dialogue shapes our actions. Be curious about your thoughts and feelings and release those that do not support your growth.

Thoughts and feelings are like raindrops. Some we let fall, forgotten, while others we taste and keep. By noticing which drops touch our tongues and which we let drop to the earth, we gain power over our inner weather. Our inner dialogue lets us choose what nourishes us, clearing the storm and cleansing our bodies.

DAY 51

Restoring Balance in Relationships

Sometimes relationships go off balance. When this happens, we can take thoughtful steps to address the challenge and seek understanding. Begin by reflecting on yourself: consider your role in the situation, the emotions and thoughts arising within you, and whether assumptions or worries are clouding your view. Ask yourself whether you truly want to restore harmony.

By honestly assessing our feelings, actions, and intentions, we gain insight to act wisely. This awareness becomes the key to unlocking our mind and nurturing a healthier, more balanced connection with others.

DAY 52

The Gift of Validation

Validating another person's opinions deepens connection and understanding. It means seeking truth in their viewpoint and showing that we genuinely want to understand, without needing to prove who is right.

When we validate others, we reduce defensiveness, anger, and tension, opening space for listening, problem-solving, and support. Validation does not mean agreement; it is a gesture of respect. By giving this gift, we nurture healthier relationships, foster closeness, and create a foundation for mental and emotional well-being, transforming both our lives and those we connect with.

DAY 53

STEP #11

Nurturing Self-Worth and Respect

Self-worth and self-respect are partners in Recovery, fueling our healing and growth. We can shift our inner dialogue from *I don't deserve happiness* to *I have much to offer, and relationships help me grow.*

These qualities can be deeply rooted in our lives, even if past influences (such as parents, friends, or coaches) taught us self-doubt. It's time to embrace our potential, recognize our value, and claim our right to healing, health, and a life filled with purpose and self-respect.

DAY 54

The Power of Awareness and Compassion

Self-awareness and self-compassion are essential in relationships. Each of us share these traits to help us validate each other's thoughts and feelings without needing to agree or even like each other.

Self-awareness means noticing our own thoughts and emotions. Self-compassion softens our heart, reducing judgment toward others. Connection is expressed through our presence: listening fully, observing, maintaining eye contact, and being in the moment. By tending to our inner world with care, we create a calm and supportive space, offering comfort to those experiencing distress and fostering deeper, more meaningful connections.

DAY 55

Authenticity and the Spirit Within

Being true to ourselves in a relationship opens our hearts to honor another's thoughts, feelings, and actions. Refrain from competing or diminishing; see the person as an equal soul, not fragile.

Embrace mistakes with compassion. Listen deeply, ask for guidance, and share advice only when invited, remembering humility in all you say.

By knowing who we are and living each moment with intention, we allow our spirit to grow. This authentic presence becomes a gentle light, reflecting God's love and inspiring those around us.

DAY 56

The Harmony of Change and Acceptance

Recovery teaches us that two seemingly opposing truths can coexist. Change and acceptance are both essential: we honor who we are while embracing growth. Life is full of contrasts: we can feel joy and sorrow at the same time or see multiple sides of an issue. Thoughts and emotions continually shift, offering fresh perspectives.

By welcoming change, we deepen self-awareness, discover the potential for growth, and awaken to the gentle call to respond with wisdom, compassion, and presence in every moment.

DAY 57

The Wisdom of Recovery Living

Recovery embraces opposites: we can be strong and gentle, desire solitude yet seek connection, share openly while keeping some things private, or disagree and remain friends.

Through self-awareness, we notice how these contrasts influence both ourselves and others. Seeing another's perspective can shift our thinking when the facts support it.

Practicing this approach can ease sadness, reduce anxiety, and curb urges to misuse substances. Even when situations remain unchanged, our spiritual growth deepens, revealing clarity, healing, and a fuller sense of peace.

DAY 58

The Gentle Art of Emotional Regulation

Emotional regulation is like a thermostat: we raise the heat when cold and cool things down when hot.

Our wise mind gently guides us, helping us master emotions, plan for challenges, act contrary to impulsive urges, and check whether our emotions fit the temperature of the situation.

By mindfully practicing emotional regulation, we are able to respond regardless of our inner temperature. This clarity allows us to interpret our internal experiences and those in our outer world. This brings us balance, understanding and calm to our hearts.

DAY 59

Healing Through Connection

Reconnecting with our feelings is a part of Recovery. Emotions from childhood abuse, a parent's substance misuse, or other distressing events can stay trapped inside of us for years.

Healing begins by connecting with healthy, supportive people who create safety so that we can release buried feelings. Like calling a plumber to unclog a blocked pipe, we may need trained professionals to help clear the blockage built up inside over time.

Recovery is messy and rarely done alone. But with patience, support, and determination, we can heal.

DAY 60

Bringing Feelings to Light

Suppressing feelings due to trauma, long-held beliefs, or past events can block healing and affect how we function today. Emotions (anger, fear, love, sadness, guilt, and more) are neutral; it is our reactions to them that shape our experience.

We can gently explore our inner world by noticing what triggers a feeling, studying how we interpret events and what physical reactions and emotions we express, and observing the aftermath of our actions. Like fishing in deep waters, bringing hidden emotions to the surface can be challenging. With patience, we learn to manage suffering and open ourselves to joy.

DAY 61

Linking Our Feelings for Strength

Recovery often brings long-buried feelings to the surface. Imagine a chain: Each link represents an emotion. When links are disconnected, we feel vulnerable, leading to freezing, fleeing, or unhealthy coping.

When an event stirs one feeling, it connects to others. Becoming curious helps us notice and sort through them. By reconnecting these links, we gain strength and clarity.

Connected feelings allow us to pause, observe, and call on our wise mind to respond with care. In this unity, we find resilience and the courage to express our wants and needs.

DAY 62

The Quiet Work of Healing

Healing stirs powerful emotions inside us that can cloud our judgment. But hidden in those moments are sacred clues to our wholeness. We may grieve our missteps, yet they are part of the journey, like failed experiments that teach more than success.

To truly heal, we need to quiet the noise. The soul speaks to us when it feels safe and secure.

We can sprint into the woods ignoring the surroundings, or we can walk in gently, sit in silence, and listen to hear the voice of God/a Higher Power.

In that stillness, healing takes root.

Truth reveals itself.

And grace begins its quiet, transforming work.

DAY 63

Naming Emotions, Finding Peace

When we name our emotions, we begin to tame them. Expressing feelings reduces their intensity and helps us respond rather than react. Emotions serve a purpose: they motivate us, communicate with others and ourselves, and prepare the body for action.

Feelings don't last forever, nor do they define us. By accepting that suffering is part of life, we free ourselves from fear of it. Noticing sadness, anger, or anxiety opens the door to healing and shifts us away from impulsive reactions toward thoughtful, compassionate responses.

DAY 64

Listening to the Voice of Emotions

Emotions help us survive. Imagine walking in the woods and seeing a bear. Fear alerts us to act and protect ourselves. Ignoring feelings can put us in danger.

So why is regulation hard? Sometimes we can't identify what we feel, or we lack the skills to manage emotions. Even hormonal changes can interfere with our impulses.

Observing, naming, and understanding emotions allows us to respond wisely. They are signals about the present moment. When intense feelings well up inside of you, remain curious to their meaning. Within that awareness lies the path to healing.

DAY 65

Letting Go of Suffering

One challenge in Recovery is releasing suffering. We may cling to it, shielding our hearts from unwanted feelings. When those emotions rise, we can feel out of control and try to block them.

As buried feelings surface, we might freeze, run, or lash out—common coping strategies to keep pain hidden. Healing begins when we find safe spaces to share our stories. Support groups and trusted connections offer that refuge. If local groups aren't available, virtual communities can help us feel seen and heard.

DAY 66

Releasing Emotional Storms

Letting go of suffering frees energy for the present. When emotions run high, our rational mind falters and we may feel an urge to fight, flee, or freeze.

Pause and check the facts. Ask yourself: *Am I truly falling apart?* Then gently redirect. Use mindfulness, soothe yourself, or engage in something that improves the moment. Remind yourself: *This too shall pass.*

Other practices like movement, art, music, or calming rituals can help restore balance. Stay present. You are safe, and this wave of emotions will pass. Healing often begins in these small, mindful steps.

DAY 67

Staying Present in Emotional Storms

Regulating emotions begins by staying grounded in the present. Start by describing the situation and rating your emotion from one to ten.

If the intensity is high (seven or above), try a healthy distraction: volunteer, take a walk, read, listen to music, shower, bake, or create. These activities offer space to breathe.

Whether emotions feel heavy or light, practice radical acceptance without freezing, fighting, or fleeing. Allow the feeling to exist, then move forward mindfully. With time, awareness and skillful action we restore balance in our lives.

DAY 68

Living by Our Values

Living from our values helps regulate emotions and shields us from pride and ego. Values often emerge from those who nurtured us (such as parents, mentors, or coaches) or from life events, even painful ones.

Ask yourself: *What do I value most?* Reflect on your actions across the years. On a scale of zero to ten, how much have you avoided building a life worth living?

Others can support us in identifying our values, but ultimately, the choice is ours. When we align with them, we feel increased peace and purpose.

DAY 69

Aligning with Our Values

Recovery invites us to list and prioritize our values. Using our wise mind, we can rate what matters most, from one to ten, then choose which values to work on.

Though implementing values may feel slow or invisible, trust your heart. Each action shapes the life we long for. Over time, our hearts will recognize the wisdom in living by what truly matters.

DAY 70

Calming the Fire Within

Emotions can ignite urges to fight, flee, or freeze. Opposite action is a skill that helps us manage these urges by doing the opposite of what the emotion drives us to do.

For example, when feeling depressed, watch a lighthearted movie; when anxious, take a brisk walk; when angry, practice mindfulness. These actions can reduce or even eliminate the intensity of our emotions.

Practicing opposite action restores balance, supports emotional regulation, and fosters self-compassion as we navigate life's challenges with care and intention.

DAY 71

Navigating Difficult Conversations

Expressing concerns with someone can feel uncomfortable, and faulty beliefs can escalate problems. Emotional regulation helps us stay calm while addressing issues. If needed, take a time out; go for a walk or practice mindfulness.

Seek to understand the situation from the other person's perspective. When thoughts, emotions, facts, and the problem align, and compromise may or may not be possible, we choose our response: solve the problem, feel better, tolerate it, release it, or step away.

Approaching concerns mindfully fosters clarity, compassion, and wise action.

DAY 72

STEP #10

Finding Clarity Through Facts

Our emotions shape how we perceive events, sometimes leading to overreactions. Checking the facts helps us manage both our feelings and our communication with others.

Ask yourself: *What emotion am I feeling? What event triggered it? What thoughts or assumptions am I making? Am I imagining a threat or catastrophe? Does the intensity of my emotion match the facts?*

Reflecting on these questions helps distinguish whether our feelings arise from past experiences or our interpretation of the present, allowing us to respond with clarity, calm, and wisdom.

DAY 73

Nurturing Joy Through Positive Experiences

Building positive experiences means inviting more joy into our lives. Playing mini-golf with a friend, getting a weekend away, fishing, or attending a play—these are activities that nourish our spirit.

When negative thoughts arise, gently return to the present moment. Mindful focus keeps attention on the pleasure at hand.

Once the experience ends, release worry about what comes next. Worry is like a rocking chair: motion going nowhere. Embrace today, savor the moment, and allow joy to guide your Recovery and well-being.

DAY 74

Living Through Our Values

Understanding our values in Recovery clarifies how we want to live. Values are standards that guide behavior and reveal what we hold most important: faith, family, courage, trust, career, or integrity.

Reflect on the values that matter to you and let them guide your daily choices. Living by our values shapes how we treat ourselves and others, creating alignment between our mind and heart. Within this alignment, we discover purpose, clarity, and a deeper connection to our true selves.

DAY 75

Healing Through Self-Awareness

Self-defeating thoughts arise from the dialogue we have with ourselves, blocking growth and well-being. They show up as self-doubt, fear of failure, perfectionism, or constant negative self-talk.

Notice what your thoughts are telling you. Write them down. These thoughts (alongside moods, mental images, or situational triggers) may serve as warnings, signaling that all is not well in our mind.

Self-awareness is the remedy. These thoughts need not control us. By seeking help, taking breaks, and focusing on what truly matters, we turn our attention to cultivating compassion, kindness, and love for ourselves.

DAY 76

Understanding and Managing Our Emotions

A stimulus is anything, internal or external, that triggers a physical or behavioral response. By paying attention to our body's sensations, we can learn more about ourselves.

Fear is a common emotion, signaling that something needs attention. That fear might manifest in a racing heartbeat, perspiration, or tension. When fear distorts our reality, opposite actions help keep us grounded. Focus on the facts, remind yourself you are safe, or speak with a trusted friend to reduce the intensity of the stimulus.

This mindful reflection can be applied to other emotions, guiding us toward calm and clarity.

DAY 77

Managing the Fire of Anger

Anger arises from tension and frustration, often rooted in hurt, fear, sadness, or shame. Left unchecked, it can cloud reason and judgment.

Anger is like water heating on a stove: simmering, we can still act wisely; boiling over, we may offend, seek revenge, or lash out.

Recovery calls us to rise above boiling over. By staying mindful and aware, we can manage anger, respond with care, and keep our hearts and minds aligned with healing, compassion, and growth rather than chaos.

DAY 78

The Power of Opposite Action

Opposite action helps when emotions or urges are unhelpful. Instead of reacting as the emotion intensifies, we choose a constructive path. When angry, take deep breaths and calmly discuss the situation; when ashamed, reach out to a friend for support rather than isolate from people.

For feelings of disgust, find one truth in the other person's words. Practice compassion and empathy, imagining their perspective. Engaging in fun or physically refreshing activities can also shift our body chemistry.

By practicing opposite action, we soften our hearts, creating space for healing and recovery.

DAY 79

Transforming Envy into Gratitude

Envy arises when we long for what others have, such as a peer further along in Recovery.

When envy surfaces, respond thoughtfully: avoid putting others down and focus on the blessings in your own life.

Cultivate opposite emotions: generosity, comfort, confidence, and contentment. Let your wise mind gently remind you, *I have enough, and I am enough.*

By shifting perspective, we transform envy into gratitude, strengthening our sense of self, nurturing our relationships, and supporting our ongoing journey of healing and Recovery.

DAY 80

Soothing the Heart of Jealousy

Jealousy stems from insecurity, fear, or concern over what we lack. It can lead us to act in unhelpful or unusual ways.

When feelings of jealousy stir, practice opposite action: release control over others, share your feelings with a trusted person, stop spying, breathe mindfully, or engage in physical activity.

Remember, jealousy often reflects our relationship with ourselves. By softening our hearts and grounding ourselves in the present moment, we cultivate self-security, inner peace, and the ability to respond with compassion rather than fear.

DAY 81

The Power and Practice of Love

Love is a force that nurtures connection, strengthens relationships, and brings meaning to life. It warms the heart, inspires smiles, and gives purpose.

Challenges arise when we withhold love or give it in unhealthy ways. Love can mislead us by enabling a person's behavior, signaling a need for us to establish boundaries or, at times, let go and move on.

Recovery begins with learning to love ourselves. As we cultivate self-love, we gain the wisdom and capacity to connect with others in a healthy, compassionate, and meaningful way.

DAY 82

Embracing Sadness in Healing

Sadness arises from loss, grief, disappointment, or helplessness and can shadow our ability to feel joy. At its root, sadness reflects grief, a natural response to life's challenges.

Allowing ourselves to be present in our sadness helps us heal, even when our hearts ache. We can nurture ourselves through therapy, mindful reflection, prayer, religious practices, physical activity, grounding exercises, or simple pleasures.

By welcoming our sorrow, we create space for emotional release and growth. Embracing sadness with care strengthens resilience, fosters self-compassion, and deepens our capacity to experience joy, love, and connection once more.

DAY 83

Releasing the Burden of Shame

Shame is a deep sense of unworthiness, often rooted in childhood or adult experiences. Toxic shame convinces us we are undeserving of love, leading to negative self-talk, substance misuse, or strained relationships.

Recovery begins with opposite action: Share shame safely with a support group or trusted friend. Avoid unnecessary apologies, and distinguish guilt from shame by checking the facts.

When you begin to feel ashamed, pause, seek inner wisdom, and listen for love, hope, and compassion. By doing so, you release the weight of your shame and open yourself to healing and self-acceptance.

DAY 84

STEP #9

Understanding and Releasing Guilt

Guilt can become excessive and irrational, often linked to anxiety, depression, trauma, or obsessive-compulsive patterns. It may make us feel like a burden, taking on responsibilities beyond our own.

Childhood trauma can leave lingering guilt, leading us to overcompensate or take responsibility for others' actions. Consulting trusted peers in Recovery can help us understand its role in our lives.

Respond to guilt with honesty: make amends when needed, honor your values, listen to your body, and then release it. Let go, find peace, and move forward with compassion for yourself.

DAY 85

Cultivating Gratitude in Recovery

Gratitude is recognizing the goodness in our lives as a gift, acknowledging God's (our Higher Power's) enduring love and mercy.

Even amid sadness, anxiety, trauma, or anger, gratitude nurtures healing. Connecting with others in a spirit of love and support creates a web of safety that strengthens our recovery from mental health struggles and substance misuse.

Gratitude is felt in the heart and expressed through humility and thoughtful action, such as inviting someone to dinner, celebrating a miracle, or simply sharing appreciation. Each night, share three things you are grateful for and invite another to do the same. This will deepen your connection with your Higher Power and foster daily peace.

DAY #86

STEP #3

Nurturing Mind and Body Through Gut Health

Researchers are uncovering the deep connection between mental and physical health. Our gut, often called the "second brain," produces 80% of the body's serotonin, a key chemical in regulating mood, sleep, digestion, wound healing, bone health, blood clotting, and sexual desire.

When serotonin levels are low, your body is more susceptible to mental and physical challenges. Addressing gut health with a doctor can lift your mood, increase motivation, and support healthier eating habits. Mindful attention to both body and mind enhances well-being, reduces mental health struggles, and nurtures a balanced, joyful life.

DAY 87

Caring for Mind and Body Amid Life's Demands

Life is filled with responsibilities and deadlines, which can increase stress. Caring for our mental and physical health helps us navigate these pressures.

If you are taking mental health medications, avoid alcohol or illicit drugs, because they can reduce the effectiveness of your prescribed treatments. Even without medications, these substances can deepen depression, anxiety, and other difficult emotions.

Engage in motivating exercise for 30 minutes at least five to seven days a week to strengthen both body and mind.

DAY 88

Stepping Toward Wellness

Mental wellness is a choice, though at first it may feel like walking through quicksand. With practice, wellness activities become steadier—sometimes joyful, sometimes difficult.

Creating a calm environment and a consistent routine helps Recovery stay on track. A healthy diet, fresh air, sunlight, taking medications as prescribed, and other supportive practices can ease symptoms of depression and other mental health struggles.

Like learning to walk as infants, we may stumble and fall, but each step teaches us resilience. Through trial and persistence, we find our balance and our confidence. Hold onto hope. Wellness grows when we choose to rise and try again.

DAY 89

Choosing Wellness Each Day

Wellness is not a single event but a daily practice of nurturing body, mind, and spirit. Just as skipping dental care weakens our health, neglecting wellness can sap our strength.

True wellness requires persistence, determination, and long-term commitment. By choosing behaviors that support our health, we face life's challenges with courage.

Each day offers us a choice: to lean into wellness or to give up. When we listen to our inner voice (our wise mind) we discover the strength to continue the journey toward wholeness.

DAY 90

Preparing for Cloudy Days

Recovery gives us the strength to follow our health and wellness plan. Yet we know cloudy days will come. The best time to prepare for them is when the sky is clear blue.

"Difficult" may look different for each of us; it could present as feeling more symptoms, missing routines, skipping social gatherings, or losing track of exercise. Naming these challenges helps us face them.

What symptoms arise on your difficult days? Write them down. Then create a gentle plan of action for each one. Preparation turns struggle into resilience, guiding us back toward healing and balance.

DAY 91

The Gift of Support in Recovery

Contrary to Western thought, we are not meant to journey alone; we are interdependent beings who need gentle, compassionate support. Society often tells us to "pull ourselves up by our bootstraps," yet even boots need a heel and sole for support and comfort.

Recovery is not a linear battle. Some days will show tangible upward progress, and others will decline into shame, guilt, and isolation. This is much like remission after an illness; symptoms can return.

When relapse happens, remember: *Be mindful of the moment.* Healing cannot be rushed. With patience and support, you will find your mood lift and be able to journey forward once more with a sense of hope and faith.

DAY #92

Walking Together in Recovery

By educating family and friends about our struggles with mental health or substance misuse, we can ease their fears and lessen their judgment. Loved ones can play a vital role in supporting the Recovery journey. Perhaps they intentionally avoid serving alcohol at gatherings or join you in healthy activities such as going to a movie or playing board games. Show gratitude for their support and help them recognize the signs when symptoms return.

At the same time, gently remind them to care for themselves. Encourage moments of rest and space so they can nurture their own well-being. Recovery is not walked alone. It is a shared journey of connection, compassion, and balance.

DAY 93

Finding Balance in Stress

Every challenge we face, no matter how large or small, contributes to the stress we carry. When that level becomes overwhelming, it can harm our well-being. Acute stress may bring a headache, while chronic stress can grow from prolonged caregiving, family conflict, or work struggles.

The key is balance: using stress as a motivator for change and learning to release the stress so it doesn't stop our forward growth. By regulating our stress, we protect our health, strengthen our coping skills, and reduce the risk of relapse.

When we find this balance, we not only ease today's burdens but also lengthen our lifespan, nurture our spirit, and walk through hardship with resilience and hope.

DAY 94

From Destructive Thinking to Healing Thinking

Destructive thinking shows up as harsh self-criticism, negativity, or distorted perceptions that bring distress and hinders our Recovery. Healing thoughts, however, draw on the power of the mind to nurture hope, strength, and renewal.

Overcoming destructive habits takes patience and steady practice. You can begin by nurturing connections, surrounding yourself with supportive people, and asking, *What is the next healthy, compassionate step I can take for myself?*

When we gently interrupt destructive thoughts, we make space for healing thinking, guiding us toward resilience, compassion, and a hopeful vision of our future.

DAY 95

The Power of Hopeful Thinking

Hopeful thinking is the practice of envisioning a brighter future while acknowledging life's challenges. It strengthens us mentally, emotionally, and spiritually, bringing light where darkness once lingered.

By replacing destructive self-talk with hopeful words, we open space for healing. For example, shift the thought "I've never done it before" to "This is an opportunity to learn." Or replace "There's no way this will work" with "I will commit to making it work."

With patience and practice, we reprogram our view of the world, discovering that hope flows abundantly, guiding us toward renewal and peace.

DAY 96

STEP #2

Whispers of the Forest

Nature offers quiet blessings to body and soul. Each step along a wooded path strengthens us, easing burdens and bringing balance. In the hush of the forest, our hearts open, soothed by birdsong, stirred by fragrance, renewed by the touch of wind and light.

The forest is a gift: always near, always free, always beautiful. When we drift from the path of Recovery, the trees wave at us to begin again, to shape a new way forward, and to rediscover the beauty that surrounds us—and the deeper beauty that lives within.

DAY 97

Movement for the Soul

Exercise blesses both body and mind, no matter our age. Woven into Recovery, it supports healing and wholeness. Movement can steady our weight, protect the heart, lift our mood, improve sleep, and balance blood sugar.

Making exercise part of daily life doesn't need to be a drastic lifestyle change. It can be a short walk with a friend, physical play with family, or gentle movement indoors on stormy days. When we keep it simple and joyful, activity becomes more than routine; it becomes a pathway to greater health, deeper connection, and renewed spirit.

DAY 98

Nourishment for Body and Spirit

Food connects us—to family, friends, and moments of life. We bake for comfort, share meals in grief, and celebrate with sweet tastes of joy. Yet sometimes eating masks our feelings. We may eat when sad, angry, or bored, or even after a hard conversation, using food as a reactive coping mechanism rather than a cultural connection or physical nourishment.

If you find yourself following these patterns, then it may be time to weave nutrition into your Recovery plan. Healthy nourishment strengthens the body, brightens the spirit, and uplifts the mind, helping us heal from the inside out.

DAY 99

STEP #3

The Gift of Health

Caring for our bodies strengthens Recovery. Choosing nourishing foods, moving often, keeping a healthy weight, avoiding tobacco, limiting alcohol, and letting go of drugs all support healing. Small steps matter, even as simple as reducing meal portion sizes, walking three times a week, or seeking help to quit tobacco.

When you stumble, meet yourself with compassion. Each effort, no matter how small, honors the body you have been given. Preserving our health is not just discipline; it is love. And it is the greatest gift we can offer ourselves on the journey of Recovery.

DAY 100

The Healing of Rest

What is the right amount of sleep? There is no single answer. Yet when we are well-rested, our minds are clear, our bodies steady, and Recovery feels more within reach. Sleep protects our mental health and helps us manage substance misuse.

Disturbed rest may come from anxiety, certain medications, or mood-altering substances. Many in Recovery face sleepless nights. When this happens, you are never alone. Support can be found in peers, physicians, counselors, or therapists who can help you create a path toward peaceful, healing rest.

DAY 101

STEP #5

The Language of Connection

Communication is how we share ideas, feelings, and ourselves. We may speak in different ways:

Passive: avoiding conflict, often with low self-esteem

Aggressive: attacking with words or actions, like a tiger

Passive-Aggressive: indirect, sarcastic, or manipulative

Assertive: open, honest, gentle, respectful, and observant

Because of mental health struggles or substance misuse struggles, we may have learned to communicate passively, aggressively, or in passive-aggressive ways. Recovery invites us to grow. Which style do you use most often? How might you shift toward gentler, more honest, and more loving communication?

DAY 102

STEP #10

Curiosity in the Dark

In moments of darkness, curiosity can guide our Recovery. By exploring our mental health and substance use patterns, we can adjust our plan and find our way forward.

All is not lost. Within our hearts and souls lie the strength and wisdom to regain balance. Let hope overshadow the shadows, reminding you of your gifts, the joy of friends and family, and the sacredness of your body. Our spiritual beliefs can touch our thoughts and feelings, lighting a path toward healing and renewed purpose.

DAY 103

Managing the Journey

Recovery is a journey, striving for a fulfilling life despite mental health struggles. It is not a cure but a path of managing symptoms with care and intention.

Relapse can occur, and a crisis plan provides a map for both us and our support network. Complete the following statement: "I will use my crisis plan when I notice these warning signs . . ." Identify activities and relationships ready to support you during a crisis.

If symptoms persist or worsen, seek help immediately. Keep friends, family, and healthcare providers close at hand for guidance and support.

DAY 104

Living with Intention

In Recovery, being intentional means actively focusing on our wellness and taking steps that support growth. Coping ahead of time with difficult situations brings this intention to life.

You can begin by writing a recovery plan: identify situations that may trigger unhelpful behaviors, choose coping or problem-solving skills, imagine the scenario vividly, and rehearse how you will respond, alone or with a trusted person.

Intentionality reminds us to pause, reflect, and act with awareness, nurturing both our mental health and our spiritual and emotional well-being.

DAY 105

The Power of Routine

A daily routine is a set of actions we repeat, like brushing our teeth or attending a support group. A routine can help us manage feelings and urges without ignoring them.

Routines differ for everyone, but a thoughtful one can reduce stress, support mental health, ease urges, and create moments to rest.

Including occasional mental health days allows us to recharge and honor our needs. These intentional pauses empower us, reminding us that caring for our well-being is both a practice and a gift.

DAY 106

The Foundation of Recovery

Building a home requires five essentials: land, foundation, walls, roof, and door. Recovery has its own five principles: values, support, security, honesty, and leisure.

Both home and Recovery depend on these basics for strength and stability. Completing a home brings joy; remaining committed to recovery brings a similar, lasting happiness.

It is not outward beauty or appearances that endure but the steady foundation of essentials and principles. When we honor our principles, our Recovery stands strong through time, opening our spirit, mind, and heart.

DAY 107

Turning Toward the Light

A spiritual awakening through Recovery is a gentle turning of the heart. When Recovery enters our lives, the darkness begins to lose its hold, not because we fight harder, but because healing light grows within us. This awakening invites us to live in a new way. Through the Twelve Steps, we begin to see, feel, and understand life differently.

This turning is daily and done intentionally by taking action. It invites the light into our fears and wounds. The light does not shame us; it frees us. As we walk in this light, we share love through our words, our actions, and our care for ourselves and others.

DAY 108

The Gentle Gift of Repentance

We are imperfect human beings. Repentance is one of the most misunderstood gifts of Recovery. It is not about shame or failure. It is a gentle invitation to turn away from harm and toward healing.

Repentance opens the door to freedom. It helps us choose a new path and release guilt. It begins with honesty, not strength. When we bring hidden places into the light, we find mercy, not punishment. Repentance reminds us there is more for us: healing, hope, and change, one small step at a time.

DAY 109

The Balance of Self-Love

Narcissism is excessive self-focus, while healthy self-love (our self-esteem) supports growth and connection. Think of it as a continuum, from unhealthy to healthy.

A balanced sense of self allows us to form meaningful relationships, develop empathy, nurture creativity, and express emotions with care. It helps us set boundaries and practice patience and gratitude.

There is no shame in healthy self-love. Embracing it enables us to shine our light in the world, honoring the unique talents we were created to share.

DAY 110

Stable Self-Love

Stable narcissism grows from healthy self-love. It shows in behaviors that are noticeable but do not harm relationships.

Our stable self-love may seek recognition moderately, accept when others do not notice, and feel neither anger nor sadness when admiration is not given. We do not expect others to read our minds and do not seek to provoke envy.

People are drawn to us for our kindness, humility, and nonjudgmental nature. Recovery offers the gift of knowing ourselves, embracing our imperfections, and connecting authentically with others.

DAY 111

STEP #6

Healing from Destructive Narcissism

Destructive narcissism is a pattern that strains our relationships, leaving frustration and distance in its wake. It includes attention-seeking, lack of empathy, shallow emotions, grandiosity, and a need to be seen as special.

Often learned from adults in our lives, these behaviors can feel ingrained. Yet, without excusing them, we can cultivate compassion for ourselves and surrender to God. Through this grace, we open the heart to genuine connection, emotional healing, and meaningful Recovery.

DAY 112

Reflections on Our Roots

Some of us are blessed with caring, compassionate parents. Others of us grew up with adults who were self-absorbed, lacked empathy, and prioritized their own needs over ours, seeing us as extensions of themselves rather than individuals.

If we were raised this way, we may notice patterns in ourselves: overreacting to minor issues, withdrawing, being overly responsible, seeking attention, or struggling with empathy.

Reflecting on our upbringing allows us to understand how these behaviors have shaped our lives and opens the door to healing, self-compassion, and growth on our Recovery journey.

DAY 113

STEP #10

The Power of Protection

Protective strategies remind us that we have the right to feel safe and to be safe. Talking with a trusted friend or family member supports this sense of security.

By staying aware of our surroundings, we can prevent others' negative emotions from overwhelming us. We pause to check our thoughts, ensuring they remain rational and constructive.

We can also visualize protective barriers (a brick wall, a shield, or a suit of armor) to safeguard our spirit from the projections and energies of others, nurturing inner peace and resilience.

DAY 114

Awakening to Spirit

Spirituality is living through prayer, action, and a deepening relationship with God, or a power greater than ourselves. From birth, we are called into relationship with others, though past experiences may make connection difficult.

Recovery helps us learn how to build meaningful, intimate bonds. As we practice Recovery, we may experience a spiritual awakening: the sun seems brighter, water tastes purer, and every sound, touch, sight, and flavor feels alive. In these moments, our hearts open, and we glimpse the sacredness woven through everyday life.

DAY 115

The Gift of Humility

Humility in Recovery is not weakness but wisdom. It means letting go of ego and pride, embracing truth, and seeing ourselves clearly in the process.

A five-year-old boy once insisted on tubing in a lake alone. When his father's grip loosened, the boy kicked free. Suddenly, a strong wind flipped the boy's tube, and his small feet stuck up helplessly. In that moment, he realized he could not save himself; he needed his father's strength.

Recovery reminds us of the same truth: we cannot walk this path alone. Humility opens the way for help, healing, and hope.

DAY 116

Healing Beyond Trauma

Childhood or early adulthood trauma can leave painful memories we would rather forget, including abuse, abandonment, or the weight of a caregiver's struggles. Trauma leaves a lasting imprint, often convincing us that suffering will always shape our future.

Yet healing is possible. When we gently open our hearts to safe people, or seek the guidance of a therapist, we invite light into the darkness. Recovery allows us to release hurt, rebuild trust, and imagine a future beyond pain.

Through courage and connection, we discover that healing does not erase the past, but it transforms the way we live forward.

DAY 117

Embracing What Is

Radical acceptance is the practice of receiving life exactly as it is, without judgment, resistance, or the wish for things to be different. This acceptance helps most in situations we cannot control, though it is less effective when action is possible and needed.

When faced with distress, pause, breathe, and notice your resistance. Allow yourself to feel pain without running from it, and gently reshape the story you tell: "Sara's behavior is out of my control, but my response is mine."

In this space, acceptance brings peace, and peace opens the door to healing.

DAY 118

When the Jar Feels Empty

Even in Recovery, there are times when our hearts feel hollow, leading to days or even weeks of emptiness. It can feel like pouring water into a jar with no bottom, our efforts draining away despite all we do.

Yet when our jar runs dry, we can turn to God, our Higher Power. His strength fills what we cannot, sealing our hearts so we never truly thirst. By pausing each day to pray, meditate, or reflect, we make space for His presence. In that sacred stillness, God reminds us that our jar will never remain empty with Him in our lives.

DAY 119

STEP #2

Recovery Is Not Alone

At times, we may believe Recovery should be a private journey. We may whisper to ourselves, *No one needs to know*, or fear others will see us as weak. Yet true strength is found in humility, the courage to admit we need support.

When we walk alongside others who share similar struggles, we discover we are not alone. Together, we lift one another, share burdens, and celebrate victories. Recovery is filled with quiet miracles, waiting for open hearts to receive them. By joining with others, we help those miracles unfold in both their lives and our own.

DAY 120

Flying with God in Recovery

Recovery leaves behind the old way of living, offering us healing and the reward of a transformed life. Though people may guide us, the true direction comes from within ourselves.

When we embrace Recovery, it takes root in our hearts. The cycle of letting go, healing, and rising connects us to God, a Higher Power who never leaves us. Like unseen electricity lighting our homes, His unseen Spirit is all around us.

Recovery invites us to soar to new heights. With God in us, we are never alone in this life.

DAY 121

Taking Action in Recovery

Recovery calls us to move beyond words into action. Sometimes we speak of change but hold back, never fully engaging our hearts and souls. Other times we take steps only on our own terms, resisting the depth of our pain. Yet true Recovery happens when we surrender fully to the process with our mind, body, and spirit.

We are not defined by our stumbles but by our willingness to learn and rise again. Each step, even imperfection, becomes part of the journey. Joy is found not in perfection but in moving forward with courage, humility, and hope.

DAY 122

A Plan to Recover

Recovery often unfolds quietly, step by step. A Recovery plan is a personal guide that helps us navigate struggles with mental health or substance misuse. It may include goals, warning signs, coping tools, support systems, and strategies for both daily wellness and moments of crisis.

Such a plan reminds us to stay active in Recovery, even when faced with setbacks. We are not defined by pain or past mistakes; we are deeply loved and created for a purpose. Let us speak this truth to our hearts often: *I have a plan to recover, and I am not alone.*

DAY 123

The Healing Power of Connection

Recovery teaches us not only how to care for ourselves but also how to extend that care to others. At times, pain can turn us inward, and we may overlook the needs of those closest to us: our spouse, children, coworkers, and friends. Yet healing deepens when we are emotionally present for others.

Relationships become vital threads in the fabric of Recovery, reminding us we are part of something greater. By saving space to listen, to serve, and to love, we nurture others. And in doing so, we find our own hearts gently restored.

DAY 124

The Quiet Miracle of Healing

Healing in Recovery is a gentle, ongoing process, a gradual restoration of mind, body, and spirit. It often appears in quiet, unexpected moments: a soft word in therapy, a shared laugh at a support group, or the warmth of being with loved ones.

Healing is rarely dramatic like fireworks; it is a subtle breeze brushing across our cheeks, a series of small, meaningful shifts. Each moment accumulates, quietly transforming us. By noticing these gentle signs, we recognize that Recovery is not a single event but a living, unfolding journey.

DAY 125

Opening the Door to Recovery

Recovery gently knocks at our heart and soul, inviting us to open the door and share our inner world. It calls us to love ourselves, show compassion, and accept our humanity, mistakes, joys, and all.

Before Recovery, we may have felt passive or defined by victimhood. Through Recovery, we find our voice, expressing our needs and desires with courage. This awakening allows us to step into a life filled with hope, healing, and wholeness.

By embracing this invitation, we learn that opening our hearts is not weakness. It is the first step toward lasting freedom and peace.

DAY 126

Companions on the Journey

A peer support community walks beside us to laugh, cry, listen, and speak truth with love. Let us seek companions who tug at our hearts, inviting us to feel life's joys and sorrows more deeply. Choose those who champion us, encouraging care for body, mind, and soul.

We need not worry about where we "should" be in Recovery. Instead, we can embrace the present moment. With trusted friends, we learn how to celebrate joy and grieve past sorrows. We will always remember our struggles, yet we can release the hold our past has on us.

DAY 127

Climbing the Mountain of Recovery

Mountain climbers face obstacles: thin air, storms, freezing winds, and little visibility. Yet they climb with radical acceptance, meeting each challenge until they stand at the summit, weary but filled with joy.

Recovery is much the same. Our obstacles may be broken connections, limited resources, or deep wounds from trauma. By accepting short-term suffering, we open the way for lasting healing. Each struggle strengthens our hearts and souls. And just as the mountaintop renews the climber's spirit, the gains of Recovery replenish our inner resolve to keep moving forward, step by step, toward wholeness.

DAY 128

The Blessing of Recovery

Recovery teaches us that our shortcomings are not enemies but invitations to grow. Through the Twelve Steps, we find healing, love, and understanding. When we stop labeling others as "they" or "them," we begin to see people, not stereotypes.

Each of us is part of a greater plan. As Recovery works within us, we heal ourselves and help others heal too. Even when we feel alone, choosing the path of faith gives us wings of hope. Recovery is our rock—our source of love, strength, and purpose—guiding us toward healing and wholeness.

DAY 129

Living into Our Name

The first step of Recovery reminds us: "We believe that Recovery is possible. With courage and hope, we commit to overcoming the internal and external barriers that stand in our way." This truth can be linked to our very names. A name carries identity, meaning, and history. It reflects who we are: unique individuals shaped by experience, temperament, and time.

Recovery invites us to embrace more than a name; it calls us to live with purpose. By opening our hearts to healing, we connect with others and grow spiritually, mentally, and emotionally. In honoring our name and our story, we find strength to serve the present and step into wholeness.

DAY 130

The Presence That Heals

In Recovery, we often hear again the call to listen for the voice of God—our Higher Power who longs for a living relationship with us. Healing is a celebration, though many have not yet experienced it. How can we walk beside them at the beginning, when there are no rituals or guides?

Step 12 reminds us that as we listen to God's (our Higher Power's) voice, we gain wisdom and walk with others on the path of healing. Recovery teaches us this timeless truth: connection with God and with one another is where healing begins and where it endures.

DAY 131

Staying the Course in Recovery

Denise had been in Recovery for two years. Her depression had lifted, her mood was stable, and she felt strong. Believing she no longer needed support, she stopped attending groups, seeing her therapist, meditating, and taking medication. Within a month, depression returned, leaving her isolated and weary.

When we begin to feel better, it is often because of the care we are receiving. Recovery invites us to adjust our plan but not abandon it. In time, we learn that desiring anything less than mental wellness is wasted energy, for healing is worth our steady commitment.

DAY 132

Breaking the Silence of Stigma

Mental health stigma is more than words. It is judgment, shame, and exclusion that wound deeply. Yet we are not alone. Healing grows in communities that listen, support, and honor our struggles without condemnation.

When faced with criticism or misunderstanding, we can bring our fears to safe spaces where compassion helps calm the weight of stigma. Each of us can also be an advocate through honesty, education, and supportive action. Together, we create understanding and hope.

DAY 133

Created with Purpose

Why were we created? How are we caring for our bodies, our souls, and the world around us? Imagine walking through a beautifully landscaped park. What do you see, hear, smell, and feel? Clearing our minds allows us to connect our senses in the present moment.

In life, we face a choice: to heal from mental health and substance struggles or to remain trapped in suffering. When we choose healing, we begin to connect to a deeper sense of self and find our purpose in life. By mindfully exploring who we are, we open ourselves to self-awareness, growth, and the person we are becoming.

DAY 134

Light Beyond the Darkness

Comfort is easy, but little grows there. Even in life's darkest moments, hope and healing remain. A couple who lost their nine-year-old child asked, "Why did this happen to us?" Seeking counsel, they turned to a priest, who saw the grief in their eyes.

He gently said, "Our Creator does not cause tragedy. If He removed your pain, He would also erase your cherished memories. Instead, the Creator invites you to lean on Him, trusting that even in sorrow, His love can bring light, healing, and the courage to live."

DAY 135

The Healing Power of Forgiveness

Mental health and substance struggles affect not only us but also those we love. At times, we may lash out, speak harshly, or neglect responsibilities, leaving others hurt and confused. When our words or actions wound, we are called to humbly apologize. Seeking forgiveness helps us release anger, fear, guilt, and shame.

Yet forgiveness is not always granted quickly. Words may come easily, but true healing requires consistent, sincere actions. Through patience and love, we can begin to mend what was broken.

DAY 136

Sacred Ground of Imperfection

Mistakes are not failures; they are invitations to grow. Each one teaches us more about who we are. By accepting our imperfections, we welcome humility.

True humility is not thinking less of ourselves but seeing clearly that we are no better and no worse than anyone else. It is the willingness to learn, to forgive, and to receive grace. When forgiveness is sought, may we respond with compassion. In this sacred meeting of truth and mercy, healing begins and humility blossoms.

DAY 137

Sharing the Fruits of Recovery

Step 12 reminds us: "We are having a spiritual awakening as a result of our Recovery. We are learning to love ourselves and practicing these steps in all of our affairs."

Recovery invites us to embrace practices that heal and sustain us, while also calling us to share what we've received. By entrusting ourselves to the Twelve Steps (or another path of healing), we give our lives more fully to Recovery. In lifting others, we are lifted. In helping them grow, we taste the fruits of our labor and continue our own healing.

DAY 138

STEP #12

Returning to the Basics

Self-awareness grows when we listen to the inner voice whispering, "You are safe. Healing is here." But as days and months pass, routines can dull our attention to the dialogue of the Spirit within us.

Keep renewal alive: read, attend a retreat, join a support group, or journal. True Recovery and happiness are not found in fleeting pleasures but in ordinary, steady practices. In the basics, we discover healing, joy, and the lasting strength to continue movement forward.

DAY 139

Healing What Was Broken

We enter life completely vulnerable, dependent on others to survive. Childhood shaped us, sometimes through love, but often through poverty, abuse, or a parent's struggles with mental health or substance misuse. Such wounds may leave us feeling unlovable, self-absorbed, or trapped in caring for others at the cost of ourselves.

The universe fractures everyone, yet healing remains possible. Small steps lead us forward. Choose compassion, practice self-care, and forgive those who harmed us. In these tender moments, we begin to mend what was broken and rediscover wholeness.

DAY 140

STEP #3

Healing Through Imagery

Imagery engages our senses (sight, sound, smell, taste, touch) and can guide us in healing past wounds. Creative outlets like art or writing offer safe spaces to process pain.

Andy was often told by his father that he'd never succeed, and he carried those words for years. Encouraged by his therapist, he drew how he wished to be treated. Through the act of creative expression, his buried emotions surfaced— grief, anger, hope—opening a path toward understanding and release.

No matter the medium of our chosen outlet, we, too, can process our suffering with creativity and open our hearts to healing.

DAY 141

Embracing Our Humanity

Healing is the journey of becoming whole again. To restore our mental health, we must present our true selves, not a mask. By exploring the depths of our souls, we confront our limitations, insecurities, and humanity. In these moments, we learn to love ourselves and take steps to live authentically.

The most profound relationship we nurture is with ourselves, embracing our imperfections, honoring our journey, and holding our humanity with compassion.

DAY 142

Refilling the Heart

Mental health and substance misuse struggles can leave our hearts and souls empty. At this tipping point, we face a choice: remain depleted or allow ourselves to be renewed.

We need not fight inner turmoil alone. Our support community can fill us with strength, and God, our Higher Power, offers energy and restoration. He invites us to drink deeply, replenishing our hearts, restoring wholeness, and guiding us toward peace and renewed purpose.

DAY 143

STEP #12

Seasoning with Compassion

A baker once made a birthday cake but forgot the salt. Guests were disappointed, and the baker realized the mistake. In Recovery, we are called to "season" others, gently sharing our experiences to show them their feelings are normal. By sprinkling in pieces of our story, we help others see that what once seemed impossible can become possible.

True charity isn't pity; it is offering ourselves fully, using our own journey to lift and guide those who are also walking the path of healing.

DAY 144

STEP #8

The Gift of Trust

Trust is believing someone is reliable and honest. Yet for many, that trust is hard-won. Past hurts and broken promises make opening our hearts risky. People will disappoint us, but accepting this doesn't mean giving up. It means embracing our shared imperfection.

When we encounter those rare souls who follow through, who are consistent and real, we call them strong friends. They remind us that trust, though fragile, is still possible and worth nurturing.

DAY 145

STEP #8

Healing Through Connection

Recovery grows through connection. Healing doesn't happen alone; it unfolds when we trust and engage with others, even when it feels risky. By building meaningful relationships and embracing supportive activities, we can release past pain and discover unexpected joy. In turn, we can give back, offering kindness and guidance to those on the same path.

Together, we can nurture love, hope, and connection, reminding one another that Recovery is stronger when shared.

DAY 146

Embracing the Highs and Lows

Recovery ebbs and flows like the waves washing ashore. Some days, symptoms are washed away, bringing contentment; other days, the waves crash into us deepening our anxiety and depression. We can honor both peace and struggle.

By staying emotionally balanced, we learn to navigate Recovery's highs and lows with grace, patience, and self-compassion, trusting that each moment, joyful or challenging, serves our growth.

DAY 147

STEP #11

The Sacred Now

If you had only a year to live, how would you spend it? One woman, facing stage four cancer, chose presence over bucket lists: cooking, loving her children, and living each moment.

In Recovery, the smallest acts become sacred: letting go, showing up, loving well. Each choice grounds us in the present, saying, "I am here, fully." Recovery teaches us to live intentionally, not perfectly, finding grace and meaning in every moment of our lives.

DAY 148

In the Beginning

Starting something new in Recovery takes courage, and courage doesn't mean we're free from fear. In fact, healing often brings fear to the surface.

Steve, recovering from trauma and substance misuse, felt overwhelmed each time he tried to attend his support group. One week, he made it to the building but couldn't walk in. The next week, he entered, shaking, and stayed.

Steve discovered that true courage isn't the absence of fear; it's choosing to move forward anyway. What carried him through wasn't willpower alone; it was the Spirit within him, gently whispering: *You are safe. You are strong. You are not alone.*

DAY 149

Carried by Clouds

Reflect on your journey. Who offered you a life jacket when you were drowning? Who deeply loved you when you couldn't love yourself?

We can find safety by placing trust in others. Fellow recoverees understand our pain. Their presence is love in action. They may sit beside us at a meeting, call to check in, meet for coffee, or pray with us.

Their support is like a soft cloud, cushioning us from the heat of suffering, catching our tears like rain, and gently clearing the sky so we can shine, rest, and find peace on this earth.

DAY 150

From Darkness to Hope

Healing comes quietly, step by step. In Recovery, we empty our hearts to uncover the root of our pain. This emptying is sacred, laying down the old self so something new can rise.

In the darkest moments, hope feels lost. But within each of us lies an empty tomb, a quiet place where a flicker of hope still lives.

The path may be muddy, uncertain, and slow. But beneath it lies solid ground. As long as we breathe, our soul can rise from the mud and walk steadily toward healing on firmer, brighter soil.

DAY 151

STEP #8

Choosing Our Circle

Recovery invites us to seek support from trusted therapists and peers who share the path. But not everyone will be safe or helpful. Be mindful of those offering quick fixes or lacking genuine care.

We have the freedom to voice what we need. By listening to our inner wisdom, we learn who is worthy of our trust.

Some connections may not feel right, and that's okay. Gently stepping away is not rejection; it's empowerment. It's honoring our healing.

Recovery teaches us to choose wisely, to protect our hearts, to set boundaries, and to walk with those who walk with love.

DAY 152

Unexpected Healing

Healing often comes in small, quiet miracles, sometimes when we least expect it.

Michael, carrying the weight of childhood trauma and depression, set out on his bike along a wooded trail, hoping nature might ease his pain. At a rest stop by the river, he paused, suffering, angry and heavy-hearted. As he sat, a gentle breeze brushed his face and wildflowers bloomed in brilliant color around him.

In that stillness, something shifted. The suffering and anger softened. Calm took its place.

Michael smiled. Healing had found him in the quiet beauty of nature, reminding him that peace can bloom in the most unexpected places.

DAY 153

STEP #7

The Healing Walk

Were there moments in your childhood when you felt safe?

Ed was born into uncertainty: his mother lost in depression, his father doing his best but stretched thin. It was his aunt who held Ed close, offering steady love, warmth, and safety. Though memories are few, the feeling she gave him remains.

When life feels heavy, Ed imagines walking beside her in nature, remembering her kindness. That simple connection grounds him, reminding him he was loved. Sometimes, healing begins by walking back to the places (real or imagined) where love first found us. Where *we* first felt safe.

DAY 154

Community Is Our Bread

Healing happens in the presence of others. While therapy and professional support are vital, much of our Recovery unfolds in everyday spaces, such as within family, friendships, workplaces, and peer groups. When we lose connection, we risk returning to isolation, forgetting the beauty of healthy companionship.

Each day invites us to engage, to show up, and to nurture the relationships that sustain us. Just as bread feeds the body, community nourishes the soul. It reminds us we belong, we matter, and we're not alone. In community, we find the strength to heal—and stay healed—together.

DAY 155

A Sacred Mission

Let us pause and reflect on our mission in this life: to seek hope, healing, and health. Ask yourself three times, *Do I commit my heart and soul to loving, forgiving, and showing compassion to myself?*

After each repetition, sit quietly for a few minutes. Listen to your body. Feel what rises.

From birth to this moment, we've been called into relationship with God, with ourselves, and with others.

Now, imagine standing at the edge of the ocean, then diving in. Let the water cleanse you. This is your rebirth. Your life. Your sacred journey.

DAY 156

The Flame of Becoming

Anguish is part of healing. As we shed old behaviors, we make room for grace and open our hearts to deeper connection with both ourselves and others.

A young woman, fresh from college, stood at the edge of the unknown. Leaving behind comfort, she felt fear, but also a quiet spark within. That spark grew, guiding her into a new life shaped by courage, curiosity, and faith.

When we imagine what's possible, we begin to believe in it. And what we believe shapes who we become.

Let go. Let the flame within grow. You were made for more.

DAY 157

A New Path of Healing

Recovery invites us to surrender our past, our will, our shame. Letting go of who we became through pain makes space for who we were always meant to be. Grace was ours at birth; healing asks us to claim it. True Recovery means redefining our freedom, our memory, and our understanding with purpose.

We're not meant to walk alone. Our shared humanity is sacred. The road will be hard, but resting is holy too. Becoming a new creation takes courage. Whatever path we've walked, we can choose now to walk a new one rooted in wholeness, spirit, and hope.

DAY 158

Let Your True Life Live in You

In Recovery, we awaken to a sacred truth: *"The life I'm living is not the life that longs to live in me."*

That moment reveals our true self—whole, alive, waiting.

Mental health struggles, trauma, or substance misuse can harden us, but deep within, our spirit waits like water in a river, ready to cleanse and revive us. Appearances deceive; the soul longs for truth, not trophies.

Recovery calls us to listen inward, not mimic others, not chase what doesn't feed us. Let your own life speak.

Let healing lead you home to who you truly are.

DAY 159

STEP #11

Let Your Life Speak

We're often asked to name our values by a church, employer, or workshop. But are those values truly ours?

Many are shaped by others: parents, teachers, or friends. Yet the values that define our *true self* rise from within. When we live by values that aren't ours, something deep inside resists, sometimes with pain, always with purpose.

Your soul knows who you are. Listen closely. Your life is already speaking.

True identity isn't found in pleasing others; it's revealed in quiet moments of honesty.

Discern. Choose. Live from your center.

Let your values align with your spirit, not your ego.

DAY 160

STEP #2

When It Feels Like No One Is Listening

One of the hardest parts of Recovery is having faith in the process, especially when we feel unseen.

Have you ever cried out: "Is anyone out there?"

Take the story of a woman in Recovery who bravely opened her heart to a peer, only to be ignored. Still, she knelt in faith and whispered, *"Please help me,"* calling out to her Higher Power for support and strength. With a rush of calm, she heard no answering words but stood with loving assurance that she was not alone.

In her vulnerability, this woman shows us that it's okay to be powerless, to be honest, to need connection. Recovery reminds us that without relationship, healing slips away.

Her story is fiction, but her struggle is real. So is the grace that meets us in the waiting.

DAY 161

The Quiet Work of Healing

Healing stirs powerful emotions and urges that can cloud our sense of reality. But hidden in those moments are sacred clues to our wholeness. We may grieve our missteps, yet they are part of the journey, like failed experiments.

To truly heal, we must quiet the noise. The soul speaks only when it feels safe and still. We can sprint into the woods, or we can walk in gently, sit in silence, and listen.

In that stillness, healing takes root.

Truth reveals itself.

And grace begins its quiet, transforming work.

DAY 162

The Courage to Be Who You Are

It takes a lifetime to become the person we've always been. Over time, we wear masks, so often we forget who we truly are. The danger is we grow used to the pretending.

Healing invites us to gently remove those masks, piece by piece. Don't carry guilt or shame; you did what you needed to survive. Now it's time to forgive yourself.

True healing doesn't come from outside. It rises from within, asking us to listen.

We are not clay to be shaped by others. We have gifts and talents that yearn to be shared openly and honestly with the world. Will we answer the call to become who we were meant to be?

DAY 163

Becoming Our Deepest Self

Clues to our true self often appear early in life. Looking back with intention, regardless of age, can reveal our hidden gifts.

Ask yourself: *Who am I? What is my nature?* Everything around us can awaken what is most alive within. True learning comes not from being told but from honoring our inner voice.

"Faking it" feeds the ego. If we deny our spirit, we feel empty. A nurse who doesn't value life may become just a caretaker, missing the soul.

Becoming our truest self makes space for joy and reveals where we truly belong in the world.

DAY 164

Come On In

When someone rings our doorbell, we often smile and say, "Come on in." Recovery knocks in the same gentle way.

When we focus only on what we lack, life can feel hopeless. The pain and fear of the unknown can seem too heavy to bear. But Recovery is always near: steady, patient, and full of compassion. It knows what we need, even when we don't.

When we open our hearts and welcome Recovery in, peace begins to grow. We stop drowning in self-pity and start breathing in hope. With a smile, we say, "Come on in."

DAY 165

The Courage to Heal

The healing journey often feels like walking through a tangled forest: dark, painful, and uncertain. Yet within this journey lies deep transformation. When we dare to look into our soul, we may find sorrow, fear, and flickers of joy.

We might ask, "Why face this pain when it feels easier to avoid it?" But healing, like cancer treatment, requires courage to face what hurts in order to live fully.

Emotional healing is a choice, one that softens the ego, opens the heart, and invites serenity. In time, the darkness lifts, and light begins to glow from within.

DAY 166

Becoming Who We're Meant to Be

Recovery is about discovering our true self, not the self shaped by "shoulds" or others' expectations.

Take time to explore your limitations and potential. Trust the insight you're gaining by being wise and discerning as you move along the healing journey.

Dare to experiment with your life. Take thoughtful risks once avoided out of fear. True richness comes from self-discovery, not approval.

We may be judged by those who think they know what's best, but this is our path.

Doubt and frustration are part of the journey. Keep returning to our inner truth. That's where the foundation of healing will always remain.

DAY 167

The Truth Beneath the Mask

Sometimes we build our lives on false bravado, hiding fear behind excuses. When things fall apart, we blame the world rather than face what's within.

Richard, a gifted teacher, wasn't fulfilled in his university role. Instead of admitting he lacked the desire (or skill) to be a scholar, he blamed the institution. He left for the right reason, but under the wrong circumstance.

His real healing began when he told the truth.

Does Richard's story echo your own?

Recovery invites us to remove the mask, embrace our truth, and stop pretending. Who we are is enough. Start there.

DAY 168

Becoming the Light

We all face moments of doubt, depression, and anxiety, but we will get through them. Self-care is not selfish; it's a sacred act of tending to the soul. Expressing our truth, resting, and releasing ego-bound burdens nourishes our inner life.

When we care for ourselves, we root more deeply in who we truly are. In that stillness, joy awakens. Then, when the time is right, we rise again, moving toward the light and away from the shadows.

It's time to radically accept this journey. Your pain is not forever. Let go and become the radiant soul you were always meant to be.

DAY 169

Walking the Way

Recovery leads us from suffering to freedom, balance, and the sacred Way, the middle path that avoids extremes of self-indulgence and relentless self-improvement. Yet the Way can feel slow or silent, deepening our frustration when healing doesn't come on our timeline.

We sit, we pray, we wait . . . and still, nothing seems to open. But a wise voice reminds us: "Even when we don't see it, much of the Way has already closed behind us."

There is wisdom not only in what happens but in what doesn't. Trust the stillness. Healing is unfolding, even in the quiet.

DAY 170

The Truth About Calling

From childhood, many of us hear, "You can do anything you want." While inspiring, this message overlooks something deeper: our true calling honors both our gifts and our limits.

Mary, placed in the wrong role, left a tech job that stifled her creativity. By combining her artistic spirit with tech skills, she flourished in web design.

John, expected to follow in his father's footsteps as a mechanic, chose instead to pursue social work, a field that stirred his heart.

Real freedom isn't doing *anything*. It's listening inward, honoring our purpose, and having the courage to follow where it leads.

DAY 171

Becoming Who We Truly Are

Recovery invites us to meet both our limitations and our longings with grace. It awakens us to who we really are, not who we were told to be. In this sacred space, we begin to feel again, to explore identity, and to shed the false ideals we've carried.

We were born with both boundaries and beauty, and when we honor both, we live more fully. Growth means we cannot stay the same. Healing stretches us—body, mind, and soul—into wholeness.

Recovery isn't about perfection. It's about becoming honest, grounded, and beautifully alive in the truth of who we are.

DAY 172

The Gift of Honest Love

Recovery teaches us to release ego, pride, and the need to prove our worth through giving. Sometimes we're called to support others with time, money, or presence. But not every offer comes from love.

When we give beyond our capacity, trying to feel needed or important, the gift becomes hollow. True giving flows from fullness, not emptiness.

Know your limits. Trust that others in the community can offer what you cannot. Burnout is not failure; it's a sacred signal. Before we give, let us be filled. From that place, love becomes honest, healing, and whole, both for others and for ourselves.

DAY 173

Faithful to Our True Nature

Recovery is not a formula to follow or a trend to imitate; it is a sacred return to our true nature. Healing means honoring both our limitations and our potential, not someone else's version of progress.

Your path may not look like anyone else's, and that's exactly how it's meant to be. Recovery is not about being "good" by someone else's standards; it's about becoming whole.

When we live in reality, we discover freedom. By recognizing our gifts, embracing our limits, and acting in alignment with Recovery, we find our life has a purpose and meaning.

DAY 174

Turn Around and Live

There comes a moment in Recovery when we turn from survival to truly living. We begin to see the world with new eyes, no longer drawn to the chaos of our former ways.

Recovery invites us to honor our true self, not by erasing the past but by learning from it. It awakens our spiritual longing for peace, clarity, and purpose.

We learn to hold life's paradoxes (healing and hurt, sorrow and joy) and still move forward.

Look ahead. Say yes to what opens before you. Let your life speak with truth, courage, and the beauty of who you're becoming.

DAY 175

When Darkness Calls

Mental health and substance misuse can feel like walking through a dark alley at night, alone, afraid, and uncertain. Whether it's your first time seeking help or our fifth, release the shame. You are not alone.

Talk to someone. Let professionals or support groups walk with you. Darkness can be a teacher, not a punishment. It calls us to vulnerability, to courage, to being fully human.

Each of our stories is different. Some struggles are bio-chemical, others situational, but all are real. Don't compare your pain to another person's. Instead, honor your truth. Let the darkness guide you toward light, healing, and a life transformed.

DAY 176

Embracing the Mystery

Mental health and substance misuse conditions defy easy answers. "Why am I suffering?" is a question without a clear solution. Our culture wants mystery to be a puzzle we can solve, but healing isn't that simple.

Recovery invites us to embrace mystery, not with passivity but with courage. It asks us to turn inward, to face our fears, and to trust the heart's quiet wisdom. Healing may take weeks or months, but light will return.

This path is demanding and has no map. Yet when we dare to go deep, the mystery becomes sacred, where pain and wholeness begin to meet.

DAY 177

The Healing Power of Presence

In emotional darkness, the right kind of support, offered gently and at the right time, can guide us back toward healing. Well-meaning words like "Go enjoy the sun" or "I know how you feel" often deepen our sense of isolation.

What we truly need is someone who dares to simply *be* with us.

Tom, in the midst of a mental health crisis, withdrew from others. His friend Cal asked to visit, bringing no advice, only presence. Cal sat quietly, massaged Tom's hands, and honored his pain without trying to fix him.

Sometimes, love means saying little and staying close.

DAY 178

The Gift of Humility

Humility is a quiet companion on the healing journey. It doesn't weaken us; it roots us. True humility gives us the courage to face our pain and the grace to hand our shortcomings to God.

Healing begins when we grow from the ground up, accepting both our strengths and our flaws. When we emerge from the shadows, we feel at home in our own skin, at home with our whole selves.

To be whole is to embrace it all: weakness and strength, light and darkness. When we listen to what aches within us, we take what once controlled us and allow it to transform us into something stronger.

DAY 179

Rooted in the True Self

What if our mental health wasn't our enemy but a friend guiding us to solid ground? Recovery invites us to come down from the clouds and root ourselves in truth, with all its beauty, pain, light, and shadow.

Healing begins when we befriend ourselves and recognize the voice within that has been calling us all along. This is not the ego or intellect but the true self, our truest companion, inviting us to live authentically, to listen deeply, and to love who we are becoming. The true self is not a distant goal. It already exists inside us.

DAY 180

Say Yes to Life

When we emerge from darkness, we begin to feel at home in our own skin and as part of humanity. We are made of weakness and strength, shadow and light. Wholeness invites us to accept this, not reject it. Our pain loses power once it is heard and honored.

Wholeness urges us to live fully. Staying focused on what's wrong keeps us stuck, untouched by purpose. But when we choose to rise, share our gifts, and enter into relationship with others, we say yes to life and discover the deep gratitude that follows.

DAY 181

STEP #11

Choose Life, Choose Healing

Each day, we're given a choice: life or death, blessing or pain. Choose life. While it may feel easier to let our struggles define us, doing so can rob us of the deeper healing Recovery offers.

Recovery invites us to *live*, not just survive. It calls us toward the life we once only dreamed of. When we commit, lean in, and do the hard work, we begin to touch the mystery of healing. And in that sacred space, we find both hope and wholeness.

DAY 182

The Courage to Rise

When we rise from despair, we find strength in community. Recovery invites us to see our responsibilities not as burdens but as gifts that come with mental wellness. Healing is a commitment to seek joy, find peace, and welcome change.

As we learn to understand our thoughts and feelings, we lean on the wisdom of our peers. Quietly, with humility, we begin to share our truth. Our stories point others toward the road less traveled. This is where courage lives: in the human heart, guiding us toward freedom from the past and into the wholeness of a life reclaimed.

DAY #183

Returning to the Heart

We are not victims of our mental health or substance misuse. We are free to create a life rooted in purpose and peace. Within us is a release valve, waiting to free us from fear and disconnection. Have we lost ourselves in the search for healing?

The world tries to define us, but our heart knows better. By trusting our inner wisdom, we rediscover who we truly are. Healing brings us home to ourselves and to others. In that sacred space, our journey becomes a blessing for both ourselves and the world we live in.

DAY 184

The Path to Hidden Wholeness

Self-awareness and Recovery walk hand in hand. Healing begins with how we respond to the world, both within and around us. Are we living from truth, or pretending to be someone we're not?

It's tempting to let others define us, but real transformation requires courage: to listen inward, to trust our heart, and to do the deep work of becoming who we were created to be.

When we embrace our inner darkness with radical acceptance, we move toward a place of hidden wholeness—a quiet, spiritual integration where healing and love take root.

DAY 185

The Only Way Out Is Through

To live in quiet desperation is to abandon our truth. As Václav Havel said, silence can mean "living a lie" and the slow destruction of the soul.

When overwhelmed, we often blame others. But the discord lives within. If we avoid facing it, we become bitter, manipulative, and wounded in our relationships.

Real healing begins by descending into our own darkness. This is not weakness; it is the path to wholeness. Positive thinking has its place, but so does our sorrow. In that quiet depth, we meet our truest self. And from that place, life becomes deeply fulfilled.

DAY 186

The Strength of Inner Security

Security is as essential to Recovery as breath is to life. It grounds our identity and self-worth. When we're paralyzed by self-doubt, we often chase roles, achievements, or distractions, ignoring the pain within.

Performing for approval can disconnect us from who we truly are, often rooted in unmet childhood needs. But the world is not our enemy. Yes, there is suffering, but it's part of life's rhythm.

When we embrace this truth, peace finds us. Peace lets us lay down our battle gear and begin creating a life that reflects our true self: whole, free, and deeply loved.

DAY 187

Letting Go of the Need to Know Everything

Do you believe everything depends on you? Many of us grew up thinking that good only comes when we make it happen. This belief creates anxiety and strains our relationships, often leaving us burned out and alone.

When we listen to our hearts, we realize we're not meant to carry it all. We have gifts to share, but we're also meant to learn, trust, and receive.

We don't have to know everything. When we let others in, we find freedom. Relying on others doesn't make us weak; it connects us to the strength we've been missing.

DAY 188

The Gift Within Chaos

Life brings chaos, and our instinct is to erase it. But the road to healing is a long journey of patience, surrender, and trust, and there are no shortcuts. When we cling to rigid control, we block the deeper work of discovering who we are.

Fear, anger, and anxiety are natural responses to life's messiness, but they need not define us. By embracing these emotions with compassion, we create space for healing.

Growth often rises from chaos. Instead of rushing to escape it, let it shape you. Within every storm lies the wisdom, insight, and grace that lead to transformation.

DAY 189

The End Is Where Healing Begins

Life teaches us that all things eventually come to an end: not just lives but also habits, relationships, and ways of coping. In Recovery, we may resist this truth, clinging to what feels familiar. Denial whispers that nothing needs to change.

But healing begins when we release what no longer serves us. Letting go isn't failure, it's faith.

Recovery invites us to unplug from pain, not just survive. When we risk trying something new, we shed old protections and open ourselves to growth. Each ending becomes a sacred beginning, one step closer to the person we're becoming.

DAY 190

The Healing Power of Inner Work

When we help others face their mental health and substance misuse struggles, they often help us in return. Avoiding connection or denying our own darkness leaves a space where fear, pride, and pain take root.

True Recovery calls us to do the inner work: journaling, prayer, spiritual connection, and honest reflection. It's not always private, but it is deeply personal.

Healing thrives in community. Join support groups like Alcoholics Anonymous, Depressed Anonymous, or Peer Recovery. In these safe spaces, we honor both solitude and shared strength, walking each other toward peace, wholeness, and deeper understanding.

DAY 191

Rooted in Courage, Not Fear

"Be not afraid" doesn't mean we're without fear. It means we don't let our fear define us. Fear visits every soul, but we are not its victim. When we face fear with honesty and curiosity, we grow.

Within us lies not just fear but also faith, love, trust, and hope. Fear (False Evidence Appearing Real) can cloud our vision, but we don't have to dwell in its shadows.

Even when our inner world trembles, we can remain rooted. From that grounding comes wisdom, healing, and a deeper presence in life.

DAY 192

Strength Beyond Our Own

We don't have to heal by our own strength alone. Our gifts can carry us part of the way, but it is relying on our Higher Power's strength that lifts us from darkness into light. Where our strength ends, His begins, limitless in love, mercy, and grace.

When we open our hearts, God pours compassion into our wounds and renews our spirit. His love fuels our healing and calls us forward.

Just as physical exercise strengthens the heart, Recovery stretches our soul. When we feel weary, remember Christ's suffering. He meets us there, offering the strength to continue our sacred journey.

DAY 193

Healing in God's Time

Healing from mental health or substance misuse challenges unfolds in God's time, not ours. Each day, we're invited to show up for our Recovery, offering our efforts and surrendering control.

Though we may resist, God never lets go. He asks us to trust that the miracle is near, even when we cannot see it. His love surrounds us, offering protection, hope, and renewal.

By faithfully receiving His grace, our hearts expand, and healing deepens. God's timing is perfect. Our job is to keep walking with hope in our hearts and be open to His love.

DAY 194

Growing Through the Seasons of Recovery

Recovery moves in seasons, each one shaping us as time carries us forward. It's not about beating the odds or winning a battle. Life holds both joy and sorrow, ease and struggle, and we're invited to grow through it all.

We don't *make* our lives; we *grow* them. Culture may tell us we're in full control, but that belief limits our growth. The ego insists we're always in charge, yet true healing comes when we release control.

By listening to the quiet, spiritual voice within, we embrace the sacred work of Recovery, and our lives begin to truly unfold.

DAY 195

Embracing the Seasons of Transformation

We all have the power to transform our lives, and with that transformation comes peace of heart and soul. But the path to healing requires courage, honesty, and perseverance.

The changing seasons mirror our journey: autumn teaches release, winter brings stillness, spring offers renewal, and summer overflows with abundance. Each phase holds wisdom.

We are never truly alone. When we open ourselves to connection with others and with our inner world, we grow. Like the seasons, we can embrace change, allowing it to reshape our lives and deepen our relationships with love and purpose.

DAY 196

Raking the Soul for New Life

Recovery brings both highs and lows. That's normal. Like autumn, when leaves turn brilliant before falling, we, too, go through cycles of beauty, release, and rest. The letting go we witness in nature mirrors the quiet shedding within our souls.

Sometimes joy visits us; other times, sadness and anger stir. Early in Recovery, it may feel like dead leaves are swirling around inside, stirred by grief, fear, and anxiety. But clearing those leaves is sacred work.

When we gently rake through our pain with honesty and care, we make room for spring's renewal. In every season, God is with us, sowing seeds of hope.

DAY 197

STEP #3

The Hidden Wholeness of Letting Go

Recovery often hides in plain sight. Life's sorrows and joys, darkness and light, death and rebirth, aren't opposites. They coexist, inviting us to embrace rather than resist them. This tension forms a "hidden wholeness" that is essential to our healing.

Like the seasons, Recovery needs both growth and loss. Autumn teaches us that to heal, we must let go. Let the dying leaves fall (old habits, harmful thoughts) and trust that new life will follow. Though our culture clings to ease and beauty, true transformation comes when we surrender to the full cycle. In release, we find the promise of spring again.

DAY 198

Summer's Testimony to Recovery

Recovery is built through small, intentional acts: attending support groups, trusting a companion on the journey, using prescribed medication, seeking therapy, cultivating hobbies, eating well, and moving our bodies. Each step is like spring's first bloom, gradually growing into the full beauty of summer.

Together, these practices form a vibrant ecosystem of healing, just as summer's greenery thrives in harmony. Wholeness is not achieved alone; it's sustained through interdependence with people and nature.

Recovery isn't automatic. It's created by daily choices. And like summer holding the wisdom of all seasons, our healing becomes a living testimony to every brave step we've taken along the way.

DAY 199

From Hesitation to Healing

Are we dipping a toe into Recovery or stepping fully in? Let's pause, without judgment, and reflect on your recent actions. Have you been all talk, or are you walking the path?

If you're trying, even imperfectly, celebrate that. But if you're stuck, hesitant, overwhelmed, or slipping back, it may be time to look deeper. Is pride in the way? Fear? The belief you must do it alone?

Our habits reveal our truth. What we do daily shapes our healing. Recovery begins when we choose action over avoidance and trust that each step forward is a reflection of what we truly value.

DAY 200

The Four Keys to Lasting Recovery

Healing is not passive. It requires action. Four powerful keys support our Recovery: **Communication**, **Attitude**, **Influence**, and **Network**.

Share your Recovery vision with others. Speak honestly in support groups or with a professional. Be open; your story matters.

Adopt an attitude of humility and growth. Recovery is more about mindset than mastery. Make things right where harm was caused. Be a student of healing.

Let others influence your path. Learn from their stories and serve where you can.

Build a network that sustains you through the highs, lows, and setbacks. These connections are the soil where Recovery takes root.

DAY 201

Facing Our Blind Spots

Recovery is a daily, intentional act of courage. Often, we carry blind spots, especially around mental health and substance misuse. We may sense the struggle but avoid naming it, fearing what others might think.

Stigma fuels this silence. Thoughts like "I'll lose my job," "My family won't accept me," or "People will reject me" take root from culture, community, or upbringing.

But healing begins when we face what we've hidden. Trustworthy people can lovingly help us see what we've overlooked. With honesty, humility, and support, we can commit to the work and walk into the light of our healing.

DAY 202

Reclaiming Curiosity

Curiosity is a gift, and in Recovery, it can be reclaimed. Abuse, neglect, or substance misuse may have blocked our curiosity, leaving us frozen in survival mode or numbing our pain with illogical thinking. But Recovery begins to heal the brain, allowing us to imagine again, explore gray areas, and see the world through others' eyes. We loosen the grip of victimhood and survival identity, making space for who we're truly meant to be.

Curiosity replaces apathy. Creativity replaces rigidity. Life replaces fear. Be brave. Get curious. Open your mind, and let healing carve new pathways.

DAY 203

This Is What Recovery Looks Like

Recovery begins with vulnerability, unraveling blind spots and managing our emotions without being overwhelmed. As we grow in stability, we release pride, ego, and old defense mechanisms. Then we become curious without shame. We notice patterns of substance use, misplaced priorities, buried pain, or how we treat others.

This awareness invites courage. By facing painful truths, we commit to living authentically. Though we may be afraid, we press forward, creating new brain pathways and embracing healing.

We don't walk this path alone. Recovery thrives in safe connections: support groups, trusted friends, professionals.

Recovery is not perfection. It's the daily choice to live whole, healed, and true.

DAY 204

Layers of Healing Through Trust

Healing from trauma requires **Trust-Based Relational Engagement**, grounded in three key principles: safety, healing relationships, and emotional regulation.

Recovery communities often serve as the first layer of safety and support, even when others don't fully understand our experience. From there, we build a second layer by assessing our whole health and create a plan of care focusing on the following areas: mental well-being, housing, finances, education, employment, and access to care.

The third layer is learning to regulate our emotions. When triggered, consciously decide to pause, practice self-care, and choose a healthy action.

These layers work together to form a strong foundation of trust, and connection that is essential to healing from trauma and building a whole, authentic life.

DAY 205

Where Faith Meets Recovery

Spirituality gives our Recovery meaning. Why does this matter? Because Recovery awakens us to past pain, present struggles, and hope for the future. In that awareness, we may wonder: *Is growing my spirituality worth the effort?*

This is where faith and Recovery intersect. Faith invites us to accept life's gray areas, to surrender control, and to trust something greater than ourselves.

Through prayer, meditation, and honest conversation with God, we access hope. When we surrender the belief that we must heal alone, we find strength, peace, and joy on the path to lasting Recovery.

DAY 206

Start Small, Heal Deep

Healing from mental health challenges, substance misuse, and trauma requires more than surface-level change. It asks us to dig deep.

Begin by identifying what truly needs to shift. Can you envision a healthier way of thinking, feeling, and living? Avoid cosmetic fixes; they distract from the real work of Recovery.

Reflect on how your past (including genetics, family dynamics, cultural pain) affects your present functioning. It may feel overwhelming, especially when multiple wounds intersect. But healing begins with one small, intentional step. Whether it's therapy, medication, or community support, choose what feels right. Trust that even slow progress leads to lasting transformation.

DAY 207

Building New Roads

Recovery reveals many paths we've traveled: avoidance, self-doubt, blame, or even the road of kindness without boundaries. But we are not bound to stay there. Healing begins when we choose roads paved with cooperation, humility, kindness, and truth.

We learn to trust ourselves, speak our needs, and believe we are enough. Even when we've taken wrong turns, we are never too old to build new roads.

The brain is flexible. The heart is resilient. Let's release what no longer serves us and walk forward, confident, whole, and open to change. Peace begins on the road we choose today.

DAY 208

Keep Your Lamp Lit

The parable of the ten brides reminds us that preparation matters. Five brought extra oil for their lamps in case the wedding party was late. The others, unprepared, were left outside in the dark.

Recovery is much the same. When we fill our lives with peace, wisdom, and supportive people, we are prepared for life's challenges. We don't scramble in crisis. We stand steady in the light.

Recovery offers more than survival; it offers fullness, connection, and clarity. Let us be like the wise brides, keeping our lamps lit with faith, healing, and hope, ready when the doors of life open wide.

DAY 209

STEP #12

The Healing Power of Spirituality

For many of us in Recovery, spirituality and religion can feel complex, especially when past wounds are involved. Yet both offer profound pathways to healing.

Spirituality is our search for meaning, purpose, and connection. Religion, when embraced, can offer shared values and tradition. Both nurture our mental, emotional, and physical well-being.

Wherever we stand (religious, spiritual, or both), the key is authenticity. What matters is how our beliefs ground us, give us courage, and connect us to others.

Recovery invites us to explore faith, finding peace and purpose through a spiritual lens.

DAY 210

Choosing What Heals

Recovery isn't one size fits all. There are many models and strategies to guide us, but what matters most is finding what truly fits *you*.

Begin by connecting with yourself. Learn to calm your emotions and listen inward. Surround yourself with trustworthy people, create a care plan, and stay open to honest feedback. Learn how trauma affects the brain, and seek tools like mindfulness, meditation, or Cognitive Behavioral Therapy.

Choose a path that helps reshape your thinking and invites small, steady steps. Add support along the way.

Healing is personal. Choose what brings you peace, clarity, and lasting transformation.

DAY 211

Courage in the Moment

When faced with crisis, gently remind yourself: *I will be courageous at this moment.* These words can provide grounding when emotions feel overwhelming.

The first step is to gather the facts. Truth can calm the storm and reveal solutions. Then, lean on your support system. Trusted relationships built before a crisis help us feel less alone when it matters most.

Courage doesn't mean we face everything alone. It means we take one steady step at a time, with honesty, connection, and faith guiding us through. In every storm, there is strength waiting to rise within us.

DAY 212

Steady in the Storm

We are always one moment away from leaning into our Recovery plan. It offers tools to carry us through anxiety, depression, and trauma.

Triggers often pull us into the past, like financial fear in adulthood rooted in childhood scarcity. Even when the facts say we're safe, our emotions may say otherwise. But mindfulness brings us back to now, clearing space for peace.

Recovery anchors us. It doesn't shift with circumstances; it remains our steady companion. When we are weak, it lifts us. When we are strong, it walks beside us. Recovery holds us steady, reminding us that *we are not alone.*

DAY 213

The Gift of Spiritual Moments

Recovery often awakens our longing for a spiritual presence. These sacred moments give us direction, comfort, and healing.

When we stay present, we may sense gentle cues from our Higher Power, guiding us toward wholeness. These moments open our hearts, helping us heal from trauma, mental health struggles, and substance misuse.

This is the beauty of Recovery: it generates hope, health, and the freedom to live fully. Spirituality becomes a life force within us.

Stay open. Healing may arrive quietly, in moments we least expect. And when it does, how awesome is that?

DAY 214

Healing the Marks of Shame

Shame and stigma can deeply wound us, especially in Recovery. They whisper, "You are less than." But that's a lie. We are created with purpose and value.

Stigma says we're judged or dismissed for our struggles. Shame says, "I am bad," while guilt says, "I did something bad." Guilt invites responsibility and healing; shame only isolates.

Peer support and recovery groups help break this cycle. If the wound is deep, professional help can begin the healing.

The antidote? Self-compassion. When we treat ourselves with kindness, we open the door to connection, empathy, and lasting Recovery.

DAY 215

Inviting Recovery In

Recovery fills our hearts with quiet confidence. On difficult days, we can choose to invite peace, gently and intentionally.

When life feels out of control, Recovery offers calm, not perfection. Even in moments of stillness when we feel powerless, Recovery is at work, creating space for something better.

It helps us navigate shifting moods and relationships with grace. Recovery never forces its way in; it waits, patient and compassionate, until we're ready.

When we open the door, Recovery meets us with truth and tenderness, reminding us that *growth begins the moment we say yes*.

DAY 216

The Balance of Self-Compassion

The cultivation of self-compassion is the gentle balance of Yin and Yang within us. Yin comforts, soothes, and validates our pain, while Yang protects, motivates, and strengthens us. Together, they guide us toward healing.

Self-compassion invites self-kindness, reminds us that we belong to all humanity, and calls us to live mindfully in the present. It is not weakness, selfishness, or self-pity; it is the foundation of inner strength. Through self-compassion, we release shame, nurture our mind and body, and open our hearts to connection, allowing life to flow with greater peace and purpose.

DAY 217

The Gentle Art of Self-Compassion

Our inner critic whispers in ways we barely notice, shaping shame and quiet suffering. Self-compassion invites us to pause, to see that we are not our thoughts. With awareness, we gently turn toward ourselves with kindness, speaking words that lift rather than wound.

This practice is sacred: each compassionate thought is a seed of healing, rewriting the story we tell ourselves. As we soften our inner voice, peace grows in our hearts and ripples outward, transforming our relationships and reconnecting us to the wholeness of our spirit.

DAY 218

A Moment of Gentle Presence

Close your eyes and place your hands gently over your heart. Feel the warmth of your touch. Notice your heartbeat—steady, alive, carrying you through this moment.

Breathe softly, letting each inhale invite peace and each exhale release tension. Whisper silently to yourself: *I am safe. I am worthy of compassion.* Allow any thoughts or feelings to rise and pass like clouds, without judgment.

This simple act of touch is a sacred reminder: you are here, whole, and loved. With each gentle moment, self-compassion begins to bloom.

DAY 219

The Power of Acceptance

Acceptance opens the door to healing and peace. When past pain triggers your present, pause, notice your thoughts, and replace self-criticism with compassion. Denying our feelings often leads to loneliness and despair.

Imagine being alone one evening, tempted to drink, weighed down by depression. Acceptance begins with acknowledging the truth: drinking is a problem. This honesty takes courage and sparks change.

Our life's quality is measured by our willingness to accept circumstances and live by the values that give us purpose. Through acceptance, we reclaim our peace and the freedom to heal.

DAY 220

Flowing with Flexibility

Psychological flexibility invites us to remain present, even when struggling with painful thoughts or emotions. Instead of fighting them, notice and release them, allowing space for healing and creative solutions.

Imagine the thought, *I am worthless.* Rather than clinging to it, picture it written on a leaf, drifting down a stream. Slowly, it floats away, your thought dissolving into the flow of life.

Flexibility frees us from the weight of self-judgment, helping us honor our commitment to Recovery. We deserve peace, healing, and the best life possible, one present moment at a time.

DAY 221

Growing Through Emotional Intelligence

Mental health challenges, trauma, and substance misuse often stunt our emotional growth, making it difficult to learn, take action, and heal. Emotional intelligence is the ability to recognize our feelings, understand others, motivate ourselves, and manage emotions with grace.

High emotional intelligence helps us notice what we feel, understand the message behind our emotions, and consider how our words and actions affect others. It allows us to face criticism without denial or blame.

Developing a strong emotional intelligence transforms our Recovery, reshaping how we think, respond, and grow. Emotional growth opens the door to healing and meaningful connections.

DAY 222

Emotional Intelligence in Recovery

Emotional intelligence grows as we heal, shaping our thoughts, feelings, and behaviors. With this growth, our relationships with ourselves and others deepen. We communicate with more compassion, clarity, and understanding.

Building emotional intelligence involves mindful communication: choosing calming words, maintaining relaxed body language, and speaking with purpose. We manage our emotions, make eye contact when appropriate, and select the right time and environment for meaningful conversation.

As trust grows, so does connection. Emotional intelligence becomes a bridge that strengthens Recovery, nurtures relationships, and allows love, honesty, and healing to flow freely.

DAY 223

Expanding Awareness Through Cultural Intelligence

Emotional intelligence deepens our self-awareness; cultural intelligence expands our awareness of others. Cultural intelligence begins with cultural humility: being willing to learn from those different from ourselves. It grows as we notice the thoughts, feelings, and rights of others and respond with empathy.

Our perspectives are shaped by time, family, priorities, responsibilities, spiritual beliefs, and our Recovery journey. By opening ourselves to the experiences of others, we embrace diversity and strengthen our connections.

In Recovery, cultural intelligence helps us move beyond ourselves, fostering understanding, compassion, and a greater sense of belonging in the world around us.

DAY 224

Yearning for True Wholeness

Yearning is the soul's restlessness, a deep desire for connection, meaning, and wholeness. In the grip of mental health or substance misuse struggles, we often yearn for what harms us: substances, possessions, or relationships that wound rather than heal. It is "looking for love in all the wrong places."

Recovery invites us to move beyond the ego's cravings and step out of the prisons we build around ourselves. By surrendering to the process, we face our fears and embrace healthier desires.

Let your yearning call you to love, to risk your heart, and to become the person you are meant to be.

DAY 225

The Power of Surrender

Before Recovery, control often ruled our lives. For many of us, its roots trace to trauma: betrayal by someone we trusted, or growing up with a parent facing mental health, substance misuse, or trauma struggles. Our responses varied. Either we fought to achieve and lead to feel powerful, or we rebelled through substance misuse, harming people, or crime. Both gave us a false sense of purpose.

Recovery calls us to humility, to release control and surrender mind, heart, and soul to God (our Higher Power). Surrender may feel threatening or uncomfortable, yet it is the doorway to healing, freedom, and a life rooted in peace and connection.

DAY 226

Climbing Toward Our True Self

Recovery begins with an honest view of our lives, like standing on a mountaintop, looking behind, and seeing our missteps clearly. Instead of feeling shame, we use them as lessons, surrendering to the deep yearning for purpose and meaning.

True healing happens at the mountain's base, where life is real and roots run deep. Recovery invites surrender, patience, compassion, and persistence. We lean on support, give healing time, love ourselves generously, and refuse to give up.

By listening to the Spirit within and engaging our inner world, we uncover our true self. We embrace our gifts, acknowledge our flaws, and walk the path to wholeness.

DAY 227

The Journey to Balance

How long does it take to find balance in Recovery? Gary's story reminds us that the journey is rarely straight or quick.

Gary endured emotional neglect, abuse, depression, and anxiety from childhood into adulthood. He struggled with an eating disorder and binge drinking, and even after seeking therapy and medication, deep depression returned. Only through facing his trauma and committing to ongoing Recovery did he begin to understand his need for healing.

Recovery is a winding path with setbacks and breakthroughs. Like Gary, we honor our journey by staying committed, seeking support, and believing healing is possible.

DAY 228

Preparing the Way for Healing

Preparing for Recovery means moving beyond contemplation; we are ready to act. We open our hearts to those who love us and guide us toward freedom.

Recovery invites us to release control and trust the process. Just as a coach trains players to carry out the game plan on their own, we must step aside from old habits and allow healing to take the lead. True growth happens when we create space in our hearts for new ways of living.

Who are the healing people in our lives? Are we letting them lead us toward peace and wholeness?

DAY 229

Trusting the Questions

Questions are a natural part of Recovery. Some of our questions are answered quickly, while others require time and patience. When answers feel out of reach, we trust that God will reveal the truth in His time.

Healthy skepticism helps us seek understanding about our mental health, substance misuse, and trauma. Cynicism, however, blocks growth and disconnects us from the healing process.

With patient hearts, honest reflection, and the guidance of peers, the truth will come when we are ready. Recovery invites us to trust the journey, remain open, and allow faith to lead us toward healing and understanding.

DAY 230

Sacred Pause

Do you feel weighed down today? Busy, restless, or anxious? Recovery offers us a sacred pause, a moment to nurture our soul. True rest is more than closing our eyes; it is soaking in beauty, feeling peace in nature, or letting art stir our spirit.

Our soul, the essence of who we are, needs this care. When we allow ourselves to rest, we honor our journey, release tension, and open space for healing. Resting the soul is a quiet act of love, a step toward wholeness.

DAY 231

The Gift of Recovery

We are living in a sacred season of change. Choosing Recovery means stepping into a new role, one that offers hope, healing, and the strength to live differently. Recovery asks us to release harmful habits (drugs, alcohol, control, or anger) and embrace life-giving practices like rest, movement, and nourishment.

Encouragement from others lights our path, reminding us that we are not alone. When we surround ourselves with supportive people and offer the same in return, we experience healing. Positivity and self-compassion allow us to walk confidently into the world, living as the person we were meant to be.

DAY 232

Recovery: A Sacred Journey

Recovery is a deeply human journey, shaped by life's storms: grief, trauma, mental condition, family struggles, or the weight of addiction. It is never a single event but an unfolding path that calls us to be courageous, present, and compassionate with ourselves. Each step forward, even imperfect, makes us stronger and more resilient.

Though we may still feel the echoes of pain, healing softens the burden, and life grows more manageable. Recovery transforms our days into a spiritual journey, where hope and joy quietly emerge, reminding us that even in brokenness, we are moving toward wholeness and light.

DAY 233

The Choice to Heal

Recovery often whispers invitations to grow, and how we respond shapes our healing. Imagine two people encouraged to attend a peer support group. One hesitates, saying, "I don't have time," but goes anyway. The other eagerly agrees, yet never attends.

Which one truly chose Recovery?

Sometimes, we are both: the hesitant soul who follows through and the willing heart that stalls. Healing begins when we honor the small choices that move us forward. Today, when guidance comes, will you listen and step toward the life your spirit longs to live?

DAY 234

Finding Joy in Recovery

"We are the voice crying out in the wilderness, seeking the invisible so we can do the impossible."

Do you feel the hope in those words? Joy often begins in darkness, the quiet place where we face our pain and discover the truth about ourselves. Recovery invites us to walk through that wilderness, letting the light transform our soul.

Chasing joy in substances, money, or unhealthy relationships leaves us empty. True joy comes when we practice our Recovery, even when it's hard. Each choice to follow the light over fleeting pleasure slowly turns our pain into lasting joy.

DAY 235

Awakening to Recovery

Some of us step into Recovery out of urgency, feeling life pressing in. Others are dragged kicking and screaming, yet deep within is a quiet, insistent desire to heal. How did your journey begin?

Self-awareness grows as we courageously face the work of overcoming mental health struggles and substance misuse. Consider Albert Einstein: As a child, he struggled. He was bullied, misunderstood, and even seen by many as a failure. Yet he became one of history's greatest minds.

We, too, can transform our hearts and minds. With the right opportunities, gentle encouragement, and willingness to act, our struggles can become the lessons of something extraordinary.

DAY 236

Embracing Peace in Life's Surprises

Deep inner peace guides us through life's unexpected turns. Joe and Sally were shocked by news of the death of a very close friend as the result of a farming accident. Anxiety and doubt filled the air. After a day of reflection, Sally said, "Joe, why did this happen?" Sometimes the hardest things in life are hard to explain.

Tragedy can open the door to love, courage, healing, and faith. True Recovery works the same way. Inner peace comes when we accept life as it is—joy, fear, sadness, and all—trusting that this deep inner peace will carry us through every struggle we face.

DAY 237

Expanding Our World Through Recovery

Recovery invites us to meet our true selves. When we disconnect, fear and control shrink our inner world. But daily connection to Recovery opens doors we once thought were sealed.

The "impossible" often whispers that we are unworthy or incapable. Yet with faith, self-trust, and the support of a Recovery community, we discover that impossibilities are only opportunities waiting for connection.

Today, reflect on where your world has felt small. Seek those who embrace your imperfections. Together, you can transform "impossible" into growth, healing, and hope, one brave step at a time.

DAY 238

STEP #10

Rejoicing in Others' Blessings

A young boy in poverty learned a priceless lesson from his father: "Be happy for others when good things happen. Envy only closes your heart." Despite having little, he chose joy over jealousy.

Recovery invites us to practice the same skill. Celebrate the progress of others without comparison. Saying, "I wish I were as far along as them," keeps us stuck in self-doubt.

When we release envy, we open ourselves to life's blessings. Rejoice in another's success, and trust that in time, beauty and growth will flow into your own life, bringing peace and renewal.

DAY 239

Recovery That Flows Into Love

Recovery is not meant to separate us from life but to help us live it more fully. Healing may require time alone, therapy, and reflection, but love and connection keep our hearts whole.

Ask yourself: *Am I sharing the love I'm discovering within myself?* Neglecting relationships can leave us isolated, while overgiving to avoid our pain can keep us stuck.

True Recovery flows into every part of life: family, friends, work, and spirit. When we nurture both our healing and our relationships, we create a life rooted in balance, love, and lasting wholeness.

DAY 240

STEP #1

The Gift of Resilience

Recovery can feel like a cure for every wound, and we may wonder, *How is this possible?* This is the quiet power of resilience: the ability to adapt, to rise after being knocked down. Resilience may show up in our minds, our bodies, or our spirits. Each time we face adversity and continue, we awaken that strength within.

We cannot rewrite our past, but resilience allows us to shape our future. Loving our Recovery enough to embrace this gift is how we heal and how we begin again.

DAY 241

STEP #6

The Courage to Release

Within us lives an energy that remembers our story, both the joys and the hurts. When we hold on to childhood pain or past wounds, that energy becomes heavy, shaping our lives in ways we may not see.

Recovery is the gentle invitation to release the hurts that weigh us down. Sometimes it begins with a single conversation, a prayer, or the safety of a trusted guide. Letting go takes courage, but each release softens the heart.

When we surrender the pain of our past, we awaken to life as it was meant to be: open, inspired, and filled with unending love.

DAY 242

The Freedom of an Open Heart

There are moments we realize our hearts have been closed by old wounds. Through the eyes of pain, life feels small, and the world reflects only our hurt.

Recovery whispers an invitation: *Open your heart.* Step beyond the story of fear and step into the truth of who you are. This truth awakens all that makes us human—our emotions, our connections, and our capacity to love.

Even when we stumble, awareness brings us home. Each time we return to truth, our hearts open wider, and freedom flows quietly in.

DAY 243

The Freedom of Letting Go

Letting go is an act of quiet courage. When we release the weight of past hurts, our hearts open to receive spiritual healing. Peace begins to settle in, and our energy shifts toward growth.

In this freedom, we rise, like eagles lifted by unseen winds. Our higher selves awaken, guiding us toward choices that nurture our Recovery. Each release creates space for strength, hope, and renewal.

Letting go is not losing; it is gaining the clarity and lightness to soar into the life we were meant to live.

DAY 244

Releasing Fear, Embracing Freedom

Fear is the weight that blocks the flow of life within us. It feeds anger, jealousy, and the need to hide from our pain. For years, we may protect our hearts with busyness or distance, believing it keeps us safe.

But freedom comes when we stop clinging to our fear and allow it to rise and pass through. Each release purifies the heart and opens us to the present moment, where courage, peace, and hope live.

Letting go is how we return to life as it was meant to be: light, free, and unburdened by the past.

DAY 245

Rising Above Fear

Fear grows where our energy is blocked and our hearts are heavy with unhealed pain. Over time, we may sink into darkness, carrying the weight of old wounds and unspoken struggles.

But freedom begins with a simple decision: *"Enough is enough."* Each moment we choose to release fear, anger, and pain, we open our hearts to hope.

Letting go lifts us higher, like stepping into light after a long night. In this space, our hearts awaken to healing, and life begins to reveal its beauty, reminding us that freedom is always waiting within.

DAY 246

The Sanctuary Within

True change begins when we feel safe enough to surrender. Security is not the walls we build to protect our pain but the sacred space where we invite God's presence to heal it.

Kathy's deepest freedom came when she stopped fighting her depression and opened her heart to the feelings she feared. As she allowed them to pass through, her body softened and her spirit breathed.

When we trust that we are held in divine safety, suffering loses its grip. In that sanctuary within, we release our pain and receive peace.

DAY 247

The Heart Beyond Success

Bob's youth was shaped by a silent longing to be seen, to be proud, while his mother's struggles shadowed the home. He chased trophies to silence his fear of failing, seeking worth through applause.

But true worth is not earned; it is a gift rooted in compassion and the grace to be imperfect.

Today, Bob embraces healing as a sacred path: to be bold enough to surrender, present enough to feel, and gentle enough to love himself fully. In this surrender, freedom and true Recovery are born.

DAY 248

The Way Back Home

Recovery is a journey, and sometimes we drift from the path. Skipping workouts, indulging in unhealthy meals, or avoiding therapy and support groups can feel like wrong turns. Yet Recovery whispers: *You can always come home.*

Healing asks us to be bold and gentle with ourselves, repaving our plan when life curves unexpectedly. Imperfection is part of the journey.

Each moment offers the chance to return, to realign with what keeps us whole. In choosing to come back again and again, we honor our courage, our healing, and find our sacred path home.

DAY 249

Grace in the Midst of Struggle

When life feels heavy and Recovery seems distant, we may believe all our efforts are failing. Yet grace whispers that healing is still at work.

Recovery is a gentle practice: nourishing the body, moving with intention, speaking with a trusted friend, resting in prayer. Each small act is a seed of hope, even on the hardest days.

When faced with setbacks, we pause, breathe, and ask God for courage and the strength to follow His will. In that surrender, peace stirs, and we remember that every step toward healing is holy.

DAY 250

The Gentle Gift of Renewal

Our human nature carries flaws, and in Recovery from mental health or substance misuse, the weight can feel unbearable. Yet hope is never lost.

When we choose Recovery, we step out of darkness into light. Each act of self-care, each prayer, each moment of honesty loosens the grip of shame and guilt.

In letting go, we make room for grace. Here, our hearts awaken, and a gentle rebirth begins, reminding us that healing is a sacred, ongoing gift.

DAY 251

Running Toward Freedom

Let us run with perseverance the race of Recovery, looking to healing as the pioneer and perfecter of our journey.

We endure the weight of mental health struggles, substance misuse, and trauma. Our hope is to break free from the chains of genetics, shame, and others' expectations.

With each step, we learn to regulate our behavior and grow into wholeness. Guided by peers who've walked this road, we stay focused on what truly matters.

There will be suffering. But if we keep going, joy may greet us at the finish line, whole, seen, and free.

DAY 252

A New Purpose in Recovery

In Recovery, we grow in self-awareness and are called to serve others on their healing path.

Mae once felt isolated and disconnected due to her mental health struggles. But through love and connection, her life began to transform. Marrying a man with three daughters gave her a sense of belonging and purpose. Now, she nurtures their growth and healing, even as she continues her own.

Recovery has come alive in her. She lives with intention, offering wisdom, strength, and love.

DAY 253

STEP #11

A Friend Called Recovery

How close is your friendship with Recovery? Is it a distant acquaintance you turn to only in crisis, or a daily companion you trust, follow, and speak with in quiet moments?

Daily journaling keeps us connected, revealing truths about ourselves and lightening our burdens. With each entry, we strengthen the bond that the Twelve Steps nurture.

Recovery promises that nothing can sever this connection. I am grateful that Recovery knows me fully with all my flaws and loves me through my community nevertheless.

DAY 254

All In for Recovery

Recovery, our friend, calls us to fully face our mental health struggles and break free from substance misuse. This is not a "toe in the water" journey; it's a complete immersion.

Ed learned this after three severe bouts of depression. Early on, he gave only part of himself to Recovery; now, he is fully committed to his mental and emotional health.

In response to Recovery's love, how can we give less than our all?

Recovery, grant us grace and courage to take up our challenges daily and follow wherever you lead.

DAY 255

The Gift of True Giving

Recovery, our faithful friend, gives us exactly what we need in each moment. We move with the gentle nudge of Recovery, responding to its blessings with gratitude and an open heart.

Recovery loved us first and continues to guide us toward wholeness. This love becomes our reason to live fully, to love deeply, and to give freely.

When we live generously, expecting nothing in return, we reflect the heart of true charity. As Patrick Madrid, an American Catholic, author, and radio host, reminds us, "True charity involves loving others who may not be likable, much less lovable—including those who don't return that love."

Through Recovery, we learn to love without limits.

DAY 256

Sharing the Love

Recovery offers the opportunity for us to heal. It gives us the ability to respond to the concrete and immediate needs of people.

Our purpose in Recovery is to carry out the threefold mission: to freely share forgiving love, to embrace the healing power of Recovery, and to receive support from peers who are also overcoming the powers of mental health and substance misuse conditions.

By caring out bold missions of Recovery, our hearts will melt away past hurts and have space to support the healing of our fellow human beings.

DAY 257

STEP #8

Blessings for the Day

Sharing our joys and sufferings creates an opportunity to be vulnerable with one another. Let go of the mistakes of the past, learn how to love yourself, and form heartfelt connections with other people.

It's easier to celebrate a marriage, new job, or blessings from the day. It's not easy to cry with those who cry, especially when confronted with our own sadness and anxiety. With that said, a family member or friend's word can comfort us.

By receiving support from caring family and friends, we are able to regulate our moods. And when we communicate our suffering in mutual vulnerability with our support system, it lightens our burdens and allows us to find blessings in our lives.

One practice to help with the heaviness of Recovery is to count your blessings. Every night, take a moment to express three blessings from the day, regardless of how it went.

DAY 258

A Place to Belong

Barb stood at the back of the room, looking lost. It was her first Peer Recovery Group. She stiffened as John gently offered her a seat. The group felt the weight of Barb's fear, sadness, and pain.

Joining a support group or sharing our Recovery means choosing vulnerability. In doing so, we open the door to healing and offer strength to others.

In our group, we quietly hold space for authenticity. Here, we are free to be ourselves, to love ourselves. And in that sacred space, we discover something beautiful: when we love ourselves, others will too.

DAY 259

The Freedom of Forgiveness

One of Recovery's greatest messages is forgiveness. It transforms us into new people, no longer paralyzed by shame, guilt, anxiety, or self-rejection. Accepting that we are forgiven is not easy.

Forgiving those who have hurt us is hard, but often, the hardest person to forgive is ourselves. Holding onto guilt and shame cripples us spiritually and emotionally.

Recovery invites us to release the weight, to embrace grace, and to live again with joy. It reminds us again and again to forgive ourselves. In doing so, we step into the freedom of becoming the person we were always meant to be.

DAY 260

STEP #7

The Healing Power of Acceptance

The heart of Recovery is belonging to a community that accepts us completely, so fully that it frees us from sadness, anxiety, and trauma.

Sam, a young man lost in darkness, faced his father's frustration and harsh words. But his mother's love never wavered.

When family love has limits, a Recovery community offers limitless acceptance. Here, no one gives up on us. Here, forgiveness and compassion flow freely.

In such a community, Sam's wounded heart begins to heal. Surrounded by faith, love, and nonjudgment, we learn we are worthy, and that freedom begins with being truly accepted.

DAY 261

United in the Heart of Recovery

Are we willing to listen to the yearning within us for true community? In Recovery, we find others who can show us the way if we choose to follow their example.

Programs can offer short-term success, but lasting healing comes when we live what we've learned and stay connected to our brothers and sisters in Recovery.

Recovery is a moment-by-moment journey. Traveling alone, the struggle can grow heavier, but when we are united in love, we find grace, strength, and purpose. Together, we serve, support, and lift one another, accomplishing what Recovery calls us to do: heal, hope, and live fully.

DAY 262

The Miracle Standing Before Us

We need not fear discussion or uncertainty. They are the runway to deeper understanding. Without open conversations about Recovery, we risk losing both growth and the trust that healing is possible.

Many peers thrive in Recovery, but Vincent resisted. He told us, "Unless I see ten people no longer needing hospital care for mental health struggles, I will not believe healing is real."

Then one day, in the group room, ten people stood. Silence filled the air. Smiling gently, they spoke in unison:

"Vincent, you are looking at the miracle of Recovery."

DAY 263

Sharing the Vessel of Our Lives

When we share our struggles and joys, a new heart begins to grow within us.

John and Mary joined five other couples, meeting monthly to speak honestly about family joys and sorrows. Their hearts were moved, both by laughter over milestones like a new driver's license or becoming grandparents and by tears over the loss of a parent or living with a mental health condition.

In sharing both joy and pain, we gain the strength to walk with others. Equal vulnerability opens the door for growth, compassion, and transformation, shaping us into a new creation.

DAY 264

Unfiltered Grace in Recovery

In a world of apps that reshape our faces and bodies, we can be tempted to chase perfection. Social media urges us to appear flawless: taller, slimmer, smoother. Yet true Recovery invites us to bring our unpolished selves. Some Recovery spaces display picture-perfect faces, but real Recovery welcomes acne, wrinkles, rough hands, and raw emotions.

We don't admire from afar; we embrace each other in love and acceptance. Like Michelangelo's art—unafraid of flaws, steeped in truth—Recovery reveals beauty in brokenness. It's not about perfection. It's about honesty, presence, and the divine molding us into who we truly are.

DAY 265

Joy After Darkness

The joy of Recovery is born from darkness, a quiet triumph over pain and sorrow. We see it when a husband, after years of watching his beloved endure physical and emotional suffering, finds relief in knowing she is free at last.

We, too, have faced seasons when joy felt unreachable, our lives overshadowed by sadness, pain, and anxiety. Yet through the grace of Recovery, the clouds slowly part. Light seeps in. We rediscover peace within our hearts, a deep, restorative joy hidden in the very struggles that once threatened to break us. This is the gift darkness can never take away.

DAY 266

STEP #4

Fountains of Healing

Whether we drink from the fountain of sadness or the fountain of joy, each sip can lead to health, strength, freedom, and hope. Joy flows easily when life is bright, when health is strong, relationships are supportive, and suffering feels distant. But sadness can leave us parched, empty, and hopeless.

Yet when we turn to our Recovery plan in faith, trusting its healing power, even sorrow transforms into courage, strength, and freedom. Recovery asks only that we embrace its grace and blessings. Boldly step forward each day with persistence. In this steadfast journey, nothing can stop us.

DAY 267

The Happiness That Lasts

Recovery invites us to fully engage in the miracle of healing, to become people of lasting happiness. Human happiness often depends on people or situations beyond our control, but Recovery happiness is different. It is built on the solid foundation of the Twelve Steps, which never fail us.

Even on our darkest days, Recovery is a steady light, offering peace the world cannot give. We may still struggle, but as we take life moment by moment, Recovery refills us with the kind of happiness that endures: deep, unshakable, and rooted in grace. This happiness is ours to keep.

DAY 268

STEP #3

Choosing Light in Darkness

When sadness, anxiety, and despair weigh us down, joy can feel unreachable. Tom once doubted Recovery could give him the life he longed for. After a mental health crisis, he chose to practice what he learned: exercising, eating well, resting, attending his group, and staying connected. "I will not fight the darkness alone," he said.

By accepting his mood and trusting hope, he found that light returned. Even in ongoing struggles, he discovered deeper joy and peace. This is the gift of Recovery; it restores life and teaches us to live abundantly, even in the shadows.

DAY 269

The Path to Lasting Joy and Peace

A commitment to Recovery brings healing, true joy, and lasting peace. In a world filled with hatred, confusion, and hopelessness, even our personal lives can feel overwhelming. The world's answers are often temporary, even harmful. But Recovery offers something deeper: connection, balance, and renewal. It draws us close to others who understand the lived experience of mental health and substance misuse struggles.

When our hearts are sad, hurting, or anxious, we can let Recovery work its miracle. By connecting with people who walk this path, our hearts can heal, and we can find the peace and joy we were created to know.

DAY 270

Healing for the Whole Heart

Recovery is more than healing from mental struggles; it is healing from the human condition itself. We all carry scars, some from childhood wounds, others self-inflicted, and still others from life's hardships.

Recovery frees us from pain's grip and opens us to receive life with a renewed heart. It mends not only the wounds others have caused but also the fractures within ourselves. In Recovery, we find enduring hope, deep peace, and a restored spirit, proof that even the deepest scars can become signs of resilience and renewal.

DAY 271

The Power of Connection

One evening while watching an NBA game, John saw a commercial urging viewers to connect with others to improve their mental health. It was a reminder that support can come from unexpected places and that social stigma around mental health and substance misuse can be reduced.

True connection means listening deeply, offering safe spaces, meeting people where they are, and sometimes giving the "gift of silence." It's about creating trust so others can share their pain. Often, people already hold the answers in their hearts; our role is to help them find their voice and take steps toward hope and healing.

DAY 272

STEP #1

Light for the Broken Heart

Many come to Recovery through crisis, moments of darkness and heartbreak. Recovery heals wounds from our own choices and from the hurts others have caused. Because people are imperfect, even those we love cannot meet all our needs.

But Recovery offers hope and light that never fail. The Twelve Steps are a trustworthy guide, showing us how to rise above pain and restore our spirit. By practicing them, we move from despair to confident hope, knowing our lives can be transformed and our hearts made whole.

DAY 273

STEP #7

The Miracle of a New Heart

Recovery gives us a new heart and spirit, softening what was once hardened. It teaches us to release anger, bitterness, and unforgiveness, replacing them with love, kindness, and compassion. In my book, *SuperHuman Being*, I share how I carried resentment toward my father for twenty-five years after enduring physical and emotional abuse. Forgiving him was a miracle. My hard heart became soft like a cotton ball.

Recovery has been transplanting hearts and transforming lives for countless people. Is there someone you still hold anger toward? Perhaps it's time to heal and let Recovery work the miracle of a new heart in you.

DAY 274

Fools for Recovery

Step 11 is not just an intention but also action. It teaches that as we listen to our Higher Power, we gain insight, live out spiritual principles, and walk beside others on the path to healing. Recovery chooses ordinary people like us to share hope and act. Some may see it as foolishness, but the message is life-changing for those in need. We may never be famous, yet we are chosen to carry this light.

Being a "fool for Recovery" isn't an April joke; it's a calling that feeds our souls and sustains the miracle within us. All-wise Recovery, grant us courage to be wise fools for a reawakening.

DAY 275

STEP #4

The Flow of Healing

Water cleanses; blood gives life. Both flow through us without judging our emotions: peace, joy, sadness, or pain. Recovery, too, renews our hearts and spirits, guiding us through life's emotional currents. Though the path can be thorny, challenges help us connect with others in their struggles.

In Recovery, healing flows through us, bringing peace to our hearts and touching the lives of fellow recoverees. Uncomfortable feelings will come, but they do not last. With the support of friends, family, groups, and professionals, we can walk through the shadows and step into the light of a new day.

DAY 276

The Truth That Lifts Us

Today, remember:

You have come far. Each step is a thread in the fabric of your resilience.

You are worthy, not for what you've overcome but for who you are—beloved, unique, whole.

Every small victory is a hymn: rising from bed, reaching out, resting your soul.

Your smile is light. Your heart, worthy of love. Self-love is not luxury. It is life.

You are enough.

DAY 277

STEP #10

Think Differently, Live Fully

Apple once challenged the world to "Think Different." Visionaries like Gandhi, John Lennon, and Martin Luther King Jr. changed culture by daring to see life through a new lens.

Recovery calls us to "Think Differently" too. Some may call it crazy, but choosing to heal is a bold act of genius. By shifting our perspective, we transform inner turmoil into hope.

Recovery invites us to live authentically, guided by our true selves, not an imitation. In choosing healing, standing for ourselves, and letting go, we open the door to greatness and the freedom to live as we were created to be.

DAY 278

The Art of Becoming

Recovery is the brushstroke that shapes us into a masterpiece. It asks us to think differently, to question what no longer serves us, to create what has never been, to seek what lies beneath the surface. It dares us to dream of what is possible and to live with the courage of our true selves.

We step into the unknown, learning to be at peace with discomfort, for it is there that growth blooms. In this journey, we are not merely surviving; we are creating a life that is bold, authentic, and beautifully our own.

DAY 279

Playing the Game of Recovery

Recovery is like stepping onto the basketball court, discovering our rhythm, our strengths, and the unique way we move up and down the court. One person may write plays with words, another with the arc of a basketball in flight. Talent looks different for each of us, but every gift can be useful, beautiful, and good.

On this court, we learn to test boundaries, set bold goals, and take risks with courage. We don't wait until we're perfect to play; we step in, even with our scars, determined to grow. In Recovery, every practice, every shot, brings us closer to mastering the game of life.

DAY 280

Now Hiring: Courageous Souls

Recovery takes grit, courage, and the willingness to imagine a life beyond today. If it posted a job ad, it might read:

Wanted: People ready to embrace hope, healing, and growth. No experience required. Support provided. Open to all. Positions are infinite. Pay ranges from nothing to inner peace and joy. Apply your soul. Begin immediately.

The choice is ours. The work may bring struggle, yet it also offers profound healing, transformation, and the chance to live fully, authentically, and with courage.

DAY 281

The Courage to Take a Chance

Every great journey begins with a leap of faith. Risk is opportunity hidden from the fearful. Facing mental health struggles and substance misuse is risky, but choosing Recovery opens the door to growth, healing, and joy.

Jen, who battled both, recalls, "I was scared, but taking a chance on Recovery brought me blessings and happiness I couldn't have imagined."

By letting go, reaching out, and embracing life fully with family, friends, work, and spiritual growth, we become a unique masterpiece. Recovery transforms fear into courage and our lives into something beautiful, vibrant, and wholly our own.

DAY 282

A Moment to Reflect

Recovery begins with honest reflection.

Pause and ask yourself:

- *Do I turn to substances to lift my spirit?*
- *Do I reach out or withdraw from others?*
- *What do I truly see when I look in the mirror?*
- *How do anxiety and depression shape my daily life?*
- *Do I act from courage or fear?*

Notice your answers without judgment. Explore what arises, read, reflect, and connect with those who understand Recovery's journey. Each insight is a step toward self-discovery, healing, and living fully, guided by awareness, compassion, and the courage to grow.

DAY 283

The Commitment to Recovery

Walt Disney said, "Get a good idea, and stay with it. . . . Work at it until it's done, and done right." Recovery is such an idea. It requires learning the process, practicing patience, and committing to effort.

In a world of instant solutions, we may seek shortcuts, but Recovery offers no quick fixes. Through persistence, reflection, and steady work without expecting perfection, the darkness within us gradually yields to light. Along the way, we may pivot, adjust, and recommit. By mastering the basics and embracing the journey, we transform our lives with intention, courage, and hope.

DAY 284

The Patience of Recovery

Recovery never moves as fast as we wish. Dark emotions, medication adjustments, and old habits may slow us or cause setbacks. At times, progress feels rapid; other times, we seem stuck. Be patient, compassionate, and steadfast. Follow your recovery plan and never quit.

Not everyone will notice or celebrate our growth. Friends, family, coworkers, and society may reject the changes we are making. This is normal.

Work diligently, practice your tools, and trust the process. Healing takes time, persistence, and faith. Keep your head up, and let Recovery transform you at its own pace.

DAY 285

STEP #4

The Melody of Recovery

Success is not perfection; it's presence, connection, and authenticity. Like a musician playing thousands of notes, Recovery asks us to stay in the moment, attuned to our inner spirit and the people we love.

Healing is more than therapy or medication; it is practice, patience, and showing up. We may stumble, miss a beat, or lose our way, but committing to our best keeps the melody in tune.

When we have done all we can to heal, acceptance of our imperfections allows us to continue, courageously and fully, composing the life only we can create.

DAY 286

STEP #5

Healing from the Heart

In Recovery, I am learning that true healing cannot be rushed. I mastered techniques, followed my plan, and trained my mind, but my heart remained untouched.

Peers in my support group urged me to feel, to speak from within. At first, I resisted, realizing my outward progress masked an inner emptiness.

Then, after a profound loss, I shared my grief openly. Speaking from the heart transformed my Recovery.

Now, I practice fully, connecting mind, heart, and spirit. Healing is no longer just technique; it is living, feeling, and embracing the fullness of who I am.

DAY 287

The Freedom of Imperfection

Perfection is not God's requirement for recovery; faith and perseverance are. When we chase perfection, we carry a boulder that crushes joy. Our Creator did not design us to be flawless but to grow, learn, and lean on Him during times of weakness.

We are not our diagnosis. We are beloved, gifted, and called to live fully. When we fall, we release shame and guilt into His hands, trusting He can turn mistakes into lessons. Recovery is not about performing without error; it's about walking in grace, one step at a time, toward the life God intends for us.

DAY 288

The Truth That Heals

Under stress, it's tempting to relapse into old patterns. Like cancer, mental health struggles can go into remission, but symptoms may resurface. Temptation tries to lure us away from truth because we want to avoid suffering.

One man, at fifty, stopped denying his pain. "No more living a lie," he said. "I want to reclaim my life." He worked hard at Recovery, sometimes slipping, but always returning quickly by practicing self-compassion and hope.

Temptation will come, but truth leads us back. Honesty with ourselves and God opens the door to healing, strength, and the life we are meant to live.

DAY 289

Autograph Your Life with Love

When we choose to enjoy life despite the weight of mental health struggles or substance misuse, we must stay committed and keep moving forward. There is no quick fix, only the steady work of Recovery.

At thirty-five, a woman once written off as a failure began her journey. She faced depression, addiction, and isolation, yet she chose to see her struggles as opportunities. She asked questions, built connections, and pushed through the hard days, trusting freedom was worth it.

Recovery is our choice to finish what we start, to create our masterpiece, and to autograph our life with love.

DAY 290

The Grace of Rest

Recovery is hard work. Between therapy, groups, maintaining healthy habits, and medication, we may wonder if slipping back into old patterns would be easier. On difficult days, we must give ourselves permission to rest, to be playful, and to fill the empty spaces in our souls with healthy habits.

John attacked Recovery with relentless zeal, every waking hour focused on getting better. Exhausted, he told his therapist about his frustration. The therapist asked, "When was the last time you had fun?" John couldn't remember.

The answer: Recovery isn't just about hard work; it's also about kindness, balance, enjoying fun activities and the grace to rest.

DAY 291

Painting Through the Darkness

Elaine lives with mental health struggles and substance misuse, yet she refuses to let them define her. On the outside, she blends into society's expectations; inside, she battles dark days that demand all her strength. An award-winning artist, she pours her pain, courage, and compassion into every brushstroke.

When anxiety, depression, and urges press in, she moves forward with the grace of a gazelle, aware of her limits and refusing to push herself into collapse. Her peer specialist, Mary, reminds her of her gift, even in her dimmest moments. In that light, Elaine transforms struggle into beauty for the world to see.

DAY 292

The Heart of Recovery

Recovery is a labor of love, rooted in compassion for ourselves. Paula, in her early fifties, describes her journey: "At first, I imagined Recovery as arriving at health and wellness. But I learned it was only the beginning."

Over time, she embraced both traditional therapy and non-traditional practices like yoga, adjusting her lifestyle with openness. "Recovery became personal, not just a prescription," she says, eyes sparkling. "After ten years, I know what to expect, and I'm learning the beauty of surrender."

For Paula, Recovery is not just becoming well; it's living with unconditional love, compassion, and gentleness in her heart, mind, and soul.

DAY 293

The Canvas of Recovery

Recovery is like painting a canvas. Every stroke, every word, maps our thoughts and feelings, revealing what is in our heart as well as our mind.

As we create, our truest emotions surface and healing begins. We do not judge the process as good or bad; we simply honor it.

The real growth comes when we surrender control and trust our soul's instincts. Letting go is hard, but in that release, our creativity flows, healing deepens, and new pathways open, allowing Recovery to transform us from the inside out.

DAY 294

Spiritual Strength in Every Path

We may be Type A (driven and ambitious) or Type B (calm and receptive). Neither is better; both offer unique gifts on the path of Recovery.

Hector, once a Type A, learned to channel his energy into Recovery, seeking balance spiritually, emotionally, and mentally. He discovered purpose through connection to God and service to others.

Jose, a Type B personality, through spiritual growth became comfortable connecting with nurturing relationships, took time for quiet reflection, and became mindful of God's presence in his life.

Recovery is both personal growth and a spiritual journey. Courage, faith, and self-awareness allow every personality to walk toward healing, wholeness, and divine purpose.

DAY 295

Perseverance on the Path to Recovery

Athletes often speak of perseverance: the courage to keep going despite obstacles. Recovery demands the same patience, dedication, and faith, even when the path is long.

Life's obstacles (childhood trauma, financial struggles, broken relationships, or loved ones still caught in addiction) may feel overwhelming. Yet Recovery is within reach. Like athletes, we need coaches, guidance, practice, and the humility to learn before taking action.

Through perseverance, we develop skills, overcome challenges, and discover peace amidst life's messiness. Step by step, with faith and dedication, Recovery guides us on a journey of spiritual, mental, and emotional growth.

DAY 296

The Power of Temperance

Temperance is self-control: the ability to act intentionally rather than impulsively. It moderates our attraction to pleasure and strengthens our will over instinct.

Trauma, mental health struggles, or past substance misuse may leave us emotionally deprived, even as adults. In Recovery, temperance shows in resisting substance misuse, pausing before reacting to thoughts, and making mature thoughtful decisions.

When you have slipped into one of these impulsive reactions, approach yourself with compassion, not shame. Awareness of these patterns is a vital step toward healing. Temperance is more than restraint; it is a spiritual and emotional practice that nurtures growth, balance, and lasting Recovery.

DAY 297

The Strength of Diversity in Recovery

Diversity is what makes us unique, including our background, ethnicity, gender, age, religion, disability, and race. It also means reaching out to those with different experiences, knowledge, and perspectives.

Building a Recovery team takes patience. Friends, therapists, spiritual guides, support groups, and coaches bring diverse skills to meet our individual needs.

Recovery is demanding, and seeking support requires vulnerability and faith. By surrounding ourselves with diverse voices and perspectives, we guide our own care, make intentional choices, and strengthen our path toward healing and well-being.

DAY 298

Daily Rituals for Recovery

How we begin, live, and end our day shapes our Recovery. Routines and rituals, both simple and spiritual, provide focus, stability, and well-being.

Start the day with gratitude, reflection, and intention. Midday, review your progress, adjust your plan, and practice mindfulness. End with an examination of conscience: what went well, what can improve?

Recovery is a daily opportunity to become a healthier, stronger version of ourselves. By embracing routines and rituals, we cultivate joy, resilience, and spiritual balance, remembering we were created to choose what nourishes our mind, heart, and soul.

DAY 299

Choosing Healing

Life leaves wounds on our hearts and souls through bullying, abuse, parental mental health struggles, or other painful experiences. If we avoid healing, peace may remain out of reach.

Past hurts can affect our relationships, leading to apathy or emotional distance. We are not alone in these struggles. Some confront the person who caused harm; others rehearse conversations as practice, preparing for courage and understanding.

Healing is a choice. By facing our pain with compassion for ourselves, we open the door to peace, wholeness, and the ability to live fully in mind, heart, and spirit.

DAY 300

The Power of Will in Recovery

Throughout Recovery, we need to learn skills and the will to move forward. Skills guide our actions, communication reduces worry, and emotional regulation tames feelings, but without will, our heart is absent from our choices.

The will must be stronger than the skill. Recovery demands perseverance and self-compassion. When urges rise and emotions surge, it is our inner spirit (our courage, faith, and determination) that anchors us, helping us weather storms, grow stronger, and find lasting peace on our journey.

DAY 301

From Saddict to Soul Free

We were never meant to be chained to sorrow. Yet pain, unhealed, can root itself deep within, whispering that suffering is who we are.

But we are more.

When we surrender to a Presence greater than ourselves, the weight begins to lift. Shame unravels. Light enters.

Every step (prayer, therapy, a hand held in fellowship) etches new pathways in our minds and hearts.

The "saddict" within loses its grip, and we rise into a life once thought impossible.

Peace waits for the willing soul.

DAY 302

Choosing Peace Within

Peace of mind is not the absence of sadness or anxiety. It's the calm that remains when we choose wisely and trust deeply. Peace grows when we let go of grudges, release past mistakes, and live fully in the present.

Accept life's sorrows without bitterness, stay connected to others, and practice love, humor, loyalty, and compassion. Balance your goals with grace and believe in God or your Higher Power. Peace is not found by controlling life but by opening our hearts to it.

DAY 303

Staying the Course in Recovery

Recovery is like driving down a four-lane highway: mostly smooth pavement, some potholes, clear skies, beauty on every side. Then suddenly, traffic stops. An accident blocks the road ahead, and we watch the other side moving freely, feeling a twinge of envy.

Jane, in Recovery from depression, lived with long stretches of wellness through healthy habits like healthy food, exercise, and connection to people. When her depression returned, she cried, "Why do the work if it still comes back?" Her therapist gently reminded her, "This mental health struggle is temporary. Like traffic, it will clear."

Recovery has its potholes and delays, but staying on the road leads us to well-being.

DAY 304

The Gift of Walking Together

Receiving support from peers in Recovery is an invitation to sit among those who understand the same storms we face. Support groups, often available in our communities, can be overlooked, sometimes out of reluctance, fear of judgment, or the belief that our pain is unique.

Yet, within these circles, we find a safe place to be seen as we truly are: imperfect, yet worthy. This can feel both unsettling and deeply comforting.

In sharing our journey, we help one another uncover our truest selves. And in that shared discovery, healing quietly takes root.

DAY 305

Starting from Here

Ask yourself: "Is my life working right now? Is it unfolding as I hoped?"

Whether our struggles are new or lifelong, we still carry dreams worth living. Past wounds, neglect, or family patterns may have shaped us, but Recovery offers an invitation to become who we were meant to be.

Age is not the measure; choice is. With honesty, we ask: "Who am I? Why am I here? What do I hope for today?"

Life may not always match our vision, but nothing is lost. We simply adjust our course and begin again—right where we are.

DAY 306

Feeding the Soul with Hope

Why care for our soul? Like a hungry stomach, it calls to be fed. When we ignore its rumbling, our Recovery weakens.

Feeding the soul with hope reminds us we can heal. Good books, uplifting messages, spiritual writings—all nourish us. Avoid dwelling on the past or painful events to long; instead, be continuously open to growth and learning.

Perhaps we must heal from wounds not of our making. Still, we choose not to let them define us.

Feed your soul daily. Consume hope. Hope shapes thoughts, thoughts shape feelings, and feelings guide the soul toward the divine path of Recovery.

DAY 307

STEP #5

Grace Along the Way

Recovery does not call us to be perfect. Our wisdom grows through action; even mistakes and relapse can teach us.

Learning happens most deeply in relationships. Surround yourself with friends or a support group who accept your missteps, offer love without condition, and help you see errors as growth.

We are not defined by recovery, illness, or relapse.

Remember, we were given unconditional love as infants learning to walk. We fell often, yet were lifted up until we found our balance. Recovery is the same. Each fall is simply another opportunity to stand and walk again.

DAY 308

The Middle Ground of Temptation

Temptation greets us daily, whether through substances, food, or neglecting our Recovery plan. Giving in may feel like relief, but it separates us from our true selves. Wisdom whispers, *Do not argue with temptation's twisted advice. Choose the next healthy step.* In those moments, reaching out to peers can restore strength.

If we stumble, we must remember that it is only a bump in the road. Making amends heals relationships, but forgiving ourselves, though harder, is the deepest act of kindness. Recovery is not lost; it is waiting for us to return.

DAY 309

Habits that Shape Our Recovery

We all carry habits, some life-giving, others harmful. Healthy routines like brushing our teeth, sharing time with loved ones, or attending support groups strengthen us. Yet destructive habits, like overeating, substance misuse, or neglecting self-care, can quietly erode our spirit. In Recovery, both kinds of habits often intertwine.

When we slip into old patterns, let us meet ourselves with compassion, not shame. Every stumble is an opportunity for awareness, and awareness opens the door to change. By noticing destructive intentions before they take root, we reclaim the power to choose healing, one moment and one habit at a time

DAY 310

The Quiet Space Within

What awakens us to Recovery? Sometimes it is loss, pain, or the weight of anxiety. Yet Recovery whispers softly: *Pause, step inward, listen.*

In the quiet corners of your home, you can create a sanctuary. Begin with ten minutes of quiet meditation. At first, the silence feels heavy, but slowly it opens like dawn over still waters. In that stillness, burdens ease, moods lift, and new energy stirs.

Our true character blossoms when we enter this classroom of peace. Here we remember: Recovery is not only what we leave behind but the sacred calm we step into.

DAY 311

STEP #11

The Quiet Power of Habits

Life begins to change when our habits change. None is more transformative than entering the classroom of silence, sitting quietly with God in prayer and reflection. Power is not the ability to control others but the grace to steady our own thoughts and emotions.

In Recovery, this power becomes courage: courage to soften the weight of the past, to embrace healing, and to nurture new patterns of wellness. In stillness, hope awakens. We are no longer bound by circumstance but guided gently toward our truest, most authentic self.

DAY 312

Conversion of the Heart

Peace begins with conversion, an ongoing turning of the heart and soul. Conversion is not a single event but a continual surrender, saying yes to our Higher Power. Restlessness and discontent often rise from the ruminations of our minds, pulling us from contentment. In silence, however, renewal waits.

The classroom of stillness invites us to listen, to release what weighs us down, and to discover peace within. Each time we enter silence, we open ourselves to growth, healing, and deeper Recovery. Here, our restless hearts find rest.

DAY 313

Loving Ourselves into Recovery

What advice would we give ourselves at the start of Recovery or to stay committed to it? The answer is simple: begin, or continue, a daily practice. The harder part is this: ask less, love more.

Barbara, who long struggled with depression and substance misuse, once frightened a loved one by not answering her phone. A friend arrived expecting the worst. Instead, she found Barbara on the deck, sunning herself. When asked what she was doing, Barbara smiled and said, "I'm lying here, loving myself."

Recovery begins and is sustained by learning to love ourselves, one day at a time.

DAY 314

The Gift of Healing

In the bible, Genesis reminds us that we are broken, yet loved. Life may have marked us with pain, struggle, or labels, but within us lies the gift of choice: the choice to heal, to love, to create. Recovery is both a quiet event and a gentle process, reshaping what once seemed impossible into possibility.

Begin simply: Take ten minutes each day to reflect, to sit with your heart, to honor your journey. In these moments, peace awakens, joy blooms, and the wounded self discovers its true strength.

Healing is not distant; it is here, waiting for us to receive it.

DAY 315

Choosing the Path of Healing

Recovery unfolds through these quiet practices. Seek wisdom from those who inspire you and adapt their advice into your own journey. Feed your mind and heart with beauty, compassion, and love, allowing spirit, emotion, and intellect to flourish. Engage fully, with intention, in every step of your healing. Discover clarity and purpose. Say *yes* to what nurtures and *no* to what harms.

Life offers choices amidst the world's brokenness, and within us lies the power to choose. Through reflection, learning, and mindful action, we walk a path of peace, growth, and continual renewal.

DAY 316

Compassion in the Struggle

Recovery is not easy. Some days, sadness, anxiety, and dark feelings threaten to overwhelm us. In these moments, show yourself compassion and love. Name your struggles to tame them, and lean on supportive others.

Dependence can be strength. Even when we take medicine, eat well, exercise, and stay connected, difficult feelings may resurface. Experiencing them again can be a gift, reminding us we have managed before and will again. Sometimes, the most healing act is patience: to wait, trust, and remember that this moment, too, is temporary.

DAY 317

A Gentle Path of Recovery

Each day, we can nurture our Recovery plan through mindful, intentional steps:

- Begin with gratitude: Whisper thanks to yourself or others.
- Reflect on awareness: Notice when you were your best and when you fell short.
- Observe significant moments: Listen for their quiet lessons.
- Seek peace: Offer forgiveness, express mercy, or give thanks.
- Embrace freedom: Let each act guide you toward your truest self.
- Lift up others: Send blessings, hold their growth in your heart.
- Close with words that inspire: Recite a meditation, prayer, or quote aligned with your life today.

In these mindful steps, Recovery unfolds and peace blooms softly within.

DAY 318

Finding Peace in Recovery

Many people have kind friends who say, "Don't worry about anything." But that's hard to do, isn't it? Worry seems built into who we are.

Step 11 reminds us that Recovery is more than a thought; it's action. Through prayer, reflection, and mindfulness, we seek guidance from God, our Higher Power, and those who care about us.

When we turn our worries over to Recovery, peace begins to grow, even when problems remain. Most of what we fear never happens. Recovery reminds us that peace is possible, and wherever we are, it's never far away.

DAY 319

The Daily Practice of Recovery

Recovery can feel overwhelming, yet it unfolds one day at a time. Focus on today—just today. Follow your plan, and honor your steps.

Like Michael Jordan, a basketball star who practiced fundamentals tirelessly, greatness grows from small, repeated acts. Each choice, each effort, strengthens the mind, heart, and spirit. Some days feel heavy, yet in persistence we discover resilience.

In the quiet dedication to basics (gratitude, self-care, connection, reflection) Recovery blooms. The path is simple, not easy, but each day we practice, we draw closer to healing, to wholeness, and to the best version of ourselves.

DAY 320

STEP #7

The Gift of Compassion

Compassion is at the heart of Recovery. Many of us carry wounds from childhood that left us with shame, driving us toward perfectionism and harsh self-judgment. Compassion whispers, *I made a mistake, but I am still worthy.*

In these moments, we discover who we truly are. Self-compassion gives us space to rest, to say no without fear, and to trust that painful seasons are only temporary. It reminds us that healing unfolds even in chaos, grounding us in love and faith for the journey ahead.

DAY 321

Just Do It—The First Step

The hardest part of Recovery is beginning. Like a space shuttle burning most of its fuel at takeoff, our greatest effort comes in that first step. Yet once we start, momentum carries us forward. Each healthy choice is an invitation to grow, blossom, and be transformed.

Missed days and setbacks are normal. We all face them. What matters is returning, again and again. Today, add one small practice to your routine. In moments of chaos, you can lean on it as proof of your strength and faith in the journey.

DAY 322

The Pilgrimage of Recovery

Life is a pilgrimage, and Recovery is much the same. The Sioux peoples teach that the longest journey we make is from our heads to our hearts. Recovery invites us into that sacred passage. Some days feel ordinary, yet within them are moments that shape and transform us. By committing to daily practices, we open ourselves to healing, wholeness, and peace.

This pilgrimage is uniquely ours, a path where both small steps and significant milestones matter. In time, Recovery carries us closer to our true selves, uniting heart and mind in the quiet miracle of becoming whole.

DAY 323

STEP #11

The Seasons of Recovery

Recovery unfolds in seasons—times of deep consistency, moments of resistance, and stretches of letting go. Some days we eagerly embrace the process; other days it feels unbearable. Yet every season carries lessons: to commit to Recovery for life, to walk with others on the same path, to pray or meditate daily, to open ourselves to growth, and to live fully in the present.

Clouds of gloom will lift, revealing beauty and hope. By "just doing it," day after day, we grow stronger, preparing our hearts and minds to face the future with courage and faith.

DAY 324

The Miracles of Recovery

Recovery is a journey of everyday miracles. We see them in support groups, in the love of friends and family, in choosing not to drink or use, and in the slow healing of old wounds. Each step forward, no matter how small, carries grace and power.

Recovery becomes our tool belt, helping us chisel away fear and erase self-doubt. In ordinary moments, beauty quietly unfolds; in struggles, strength is revealed. We are living miracles, created to grow, to love, and to transform the world around us.

DAY 325

Packing Light for the Journey

Life's seasons of change push us through times of struggle, resistance, surrender, and growth. Recovery often mirrors this rhythm. Like travelers who overpack, we carry more supplies than we truly need. Each journey teaches us that lighter is better, yet we often forget and pick up the load again repeating the familiar patterns of the past. Over time, though, we learn to overcome what weighs us down.

Recovery invites us to trust that we need less than we imagine, and in letting go, we find freedom, peace, and the joy of being transformed.

DAY 326

when the Screen Freezes

Some days in Recovery, we question whether the effort is worth it. We feel drained, unmotivated, unable to focus, our minds heavy with sadness or unexplained darkness. Like a computer screen that suddenly freezes, our thoughts stop us from moving freely.

In these moments, it helps to remember that we are not broken. We are human. Sometimes all we can do is rest, reach out, or keep to our routine. Healing means honoring our feelings without judgment, trusting that tomorrow may bring light. Even in the stillness, we are worthy of care and compassion.

DAY 327

When the Waters Feel Deep

Recovery can sometimes feel overwhelming, as if we are drowning despite our best efforts. Dark moments may come even when we follow our plan, leaving us asking, "Why me?" Like a swimmer fighting to stay afloat, we grow weary.

Mental health and substance misuse challenges are real, often biological, and not our fault. In those moments, acceptance and patience matter. Light may return in an hour, a day, or later still. Speaking honestly with someone who listens without judgment can bring comfort. Even when we are treading water, we are not alone. Hope waits quietly to rise again.

DAY 328

Permission to Enjoy

Recovery can feel consuming, leaving us unsure how to enjoy life's simple pleasures. As a young boy, Brian loved watching sports on TV, but many times his father saw it as a waste of time and put him to work. As an adult, Brian struggles to relax, telling himself, *Don't be lazy.*

Many of us carry similar imprints, believing we don't deserve joy. Yet pleasure restores our well-being. Whether it's watching a sunset, laughing with a friend, or enjoying a favorite show, these moments remind us we are alive. Play and pleasure are not luxuries; they are healing gifts. Give yourself permission to embrace them without guilt.

DAY 329

The Nature of Our Struggle

Some people believe mental health struggles or substance use can be "cured," yet for many of us, the journey is lifelong. While trauma or life events may play a role, sometimes the root is biological, woven into us from childhood. Discovering this truth can take years, but it also gives us direction.

With the help of psychiatrists, therapy, and support, balance becomes possible. Living with symptoms does not mean living without hope. Recovery invites us into strength, purpose, and meaning. Even when challenges remain, life can still hold joy, connection, and healing.

DAY 330

Transforming Our Thoughts

At times, no matter how hard we try, negative thoughts seem unshakable. These Automatic Negative Thoughts (ANTs), often rooted in childhood, can fill us with fear, sadness, or anxiety. Awareness itself is healing, reminding us these thoughts are temporary. Our minds repeat old patterns, but we are not powerless.

By reframing ANTs into Positive Empowering Thoughts (PETs), we shift toward hope and truth. This takes patience and practice, yet over time we find freedom. Even when shadows arise, we can care for ourselves, rest, and trust that light will return. Transformation begins with compassion for our own mind.

DAY 331

Nurturing the New Within

Healing begins when we free our mind, heart, and soul to the growth already within us. Our role is to allow it to surface through self-care, joy, and love. On difficult days, instead of pushing through as we once did, we can pause and nurture ourselves. Affirm, "I honor my inner self by being compassionate with where I am today."

Each small act (walking, repeating affirmations, attending a support group) feeds Recovery. On good days, continue these practices so that when challenges arise, you can respond with compassion, faith, and the behaviors that bring true healing.

DAY 332

The Treasure of True Self

Before Recovery, we may have believed our worth was found in titles, talents, or outward success. Yet these things cannot heal the emptiness within. John appeared strong and accomplished, but years of hidden pain and trauma left him hollow inside. When his burdens finally surfaced, he discovered the courage to seek healing and truth.

Recovery invites us to do the same: to lay down false identities and embrace who we truly are. Like a sacred treasure hunt, God leads us toward wholeness, deeper meaning, and the freedom to live as our authentic selves.

DAY 333

STEP #3

Strength in the Small Steps

Recovery is often shaped in quiet, unseen ways. Taking medication, showing up to support groups, practicing daily habits—these steady choices may feel ordinary, but they build extraordinary strength within us.

On the days when life feels calm, these practices root us in peace. And when challenges come, we find we are steadier than we thought, prepared to face them with courage.

Each small step matters. Each faithful act of care is healing. In time, we discover that what once felt impossible becomes possible, because we have been gently growing stronger all along.

DAY 334

Choosing the Path of Truth

At times we face a choice: hide our struggles or courageously face them.

Tom, a respected social worker, seemed successful to everyone around him. Yet inside, depression and anxiety weighed heavily on his soul. For years, he ignored the darkness, until it overflowed and could no longer be contained.

With the support of his compassionate wife, Tom chose a new path, leaving behind outward validation to focus on healing. He embraced the pain, faced his truth, and began to be transformed. His journey reminds us that when we choose honesty and healing, hope and wholeness follow.

DAY 335

A Spirit That Moves Us Forward

Admitting we are powerless over mental health struggles or substance misuse takes deep courage. Some days, like Phil, we may dread waking up, longing to roll over and avoid another heavy day. Yet even in that darkness, a quiet spirit within urges us forward.

Phil keeps simple routines like waking, brushing his teeth, and sipping coffee, even as a cloud lingers. Each small step becomes an act of hope. By naming our struggles and admitting our powerlessness, we open ourselves to grace, healing, and the possibility of new life. Within us, the Spirit keeps whispering: *Keep moving forward.*

DAY 336

Standing on Solid Ground

Depression, anxiety, and substance misuse can feel like end-lessly treading water, struggling just to stay afloat. Recovery invites us to stop exhausting ourselves and discover the firm ground beneath our feet.

At times, we may feel we are sinking, gasping for air, unsure if healing is possible. Yet suddenly, we find our-selves in shallower waters, able to stand and take slow steps toward the shore.

When we accept our struggles, we gain a new perspective, a path toward healing and service. Take the risk to reach out, seek fellowship, and remember: you are not meant to walk alone.

DAY 337

Acceptance Through God's Grace

True Recovery calls us to acceptance, not as resignation but as surrender to God's grace. We cannot change the past or the harm done to us, but we can release the weight of bitterness and allow God to transform our pain into healing.

Life's struggles often feel unfair, yet within them we are invited to discover trust in a power greater than ourselves. As we draw near to God, we find peace, courage, and understanding.

In acceptance, we are freed—freed to love ourselves, to make healthier choices, and to walk with others toward hope and new life.

DAY 338

Faith at the Plate

Some days, even simple tasks feel heavy, and negative thoughts whisper, *I am not enough.* Yet these moments are part of the journey, not our identity.

Recovery is like stepping to the plate in baseball: We are rookies at first, missing swings, yet each attempt we persevere and eventually get better. With faith in our potential, persistence becomes prayer in action. By showing up daily and practicing our skills, we move closer to the life of hope, peace, and wholeness we are meant to live.

DAY 339

Vulnerability as a Path to Wholeness

Recovery invites us to vulnerability: the courage to feel our pain, release false images, and embrace uncertainty. This openness is a spiritual practice, allowing God to meet us where we are.

By admitting our flaws and struggles, we stop hurting ourselves and others and begin to experience true connection, love, and healing. We are not worthy of Recovery because we are perfect but because we are human.

Saying, "I am flawed, yet loved," opens our hearts to grace, freedom, and the path toward wholeness and authentic living.

DAY 340

Surrendering to Heal

Recovery asks us to surrender, to be vulnerable, honest, and gentle with ourselves. Feeling anger, sadness, or frustration does not mean we are failing; it means we are human.

Through support, therapy, prayer, and daily practices, we begin to reclaim our lives and restore hope. Accepting our mental health and substance struggles is not weakness. It is courage, a way to open our hearts to God's grace.

By surrendering and trusting in a power greater than ourselves, we find the strength to manage symptoms, embrace healing, and step fully into the life we are meant to live.

DAY 341

Courage in the Healing Journey

Deciding to heal can shift how we see ourselves, revealing courage in our Recovery. Some may need medication, some may not, but all benefit from mindful self-talk. Negative thoughts can undermine progress, even with treatment.

Loving ourselves, practicing compassion, and embracing our strengths instead of our shortcomings allows true healing to be ongoing. Connecting with peers helps us learn how others navigate pain and find hope. Don't wait to feel better. Take action today. By following a plan of care, showing up for ourselves, and seeking support, we open the path toward peace, growth, and lasting Recovery.

DAY 342

Embracing Joy in Recovery

Recovery invites openness to grow, learn, and feel fully. Sometimes, even good fortune can trigger worry, wondering when the next shoe will drop. This reminds us that feeling good can be uncomfortable, but allowing ourselves to experience joy, gratitude, and peace is part of healing. Recovery teaches us to embrace happiness without fear, to sit with positive energy, and to trust that we are worthy of life's blessings.

Go ahead—let yourself feel joy. It is part of the journey.

DAY 343

STEP #11

Choosing Joy and Hope

Recovery begins when we choose to step out of darkness and connect with others. Progress may be slow, but over time we feel, act, and even appear differently: calmer, brighter, and more alive.

We are more than any label: "depressive," "bipolar," or "alcoholic." Diagnoses do not define our worth or limit our potential. By practicing mindfulness, joining support groups, and replacing negative thoughts with positive ones, we cultivate skills and resilience.

Hope is within our hands. We can choose a life of purpose and meaning, embracing our struggles while stepping fully into joy and connection.

DAY 344

Love and Respect Through Conflict

When hurt arises in relationships, it can strain our connection with loved ones. A couple faced conflict over whether to help their adult child pay for a sick pet's care. Each parent had strong feelings, shaped by frustration and past experiences.

By calmly sharing their thoughts and listening to each other, they reached separate conclusions without disrespecting one another. Their love and mutual respect shone through, strengthened by their mental health journeys and the guidance of the Twelve Steps.

Even in conflict, Recovery and compassion allow relationships to grow with understanding, patience, and grace.

DAY 345

The SuperHuman Gift of Recovery

Recovery brings both successes and setbacks, yet it offers the profound gift of wholeness. Choosing this path makes us a "SuperHuman Being," not for fame or recognition but for courage in facing our demons, urges, and struggles.

While society applauds achievements in sports, politics, or business, Recovery asks something greater: embracing a difficult road with patience, perseverance, and gratitude. Celebrate each step forward, no matter how small. Even without awards or applause, through Recovery, we become whole, healed, and capable of experiencing life's everyday miracles.

Gentleness with ourselves is part of this sacred journey.

DAY 346

Seeing God's Beauty in Recovery

In Recovery, it's easy to dwell on our pain. Yet God calls us to notice the beauty around us—in our relationships, our children, our friends, and the world we inhabit.

Ask yourself: *How do these people or places bring me joy, support, or comfort? How can I care for them in return?*

By gently placing our suffering in a mental box for a moment, we open our hearts to gratitude and divine presence. Recognizing God's gifts in daily life nurtures healing, hope, and a deeper connection to the life and love that surrounds us.

DAY 347

STEP #3

Stepping Out of the Vault

Recovery asks us to leave the vault of our mental health struggles or substance misuse, a place of safety and predictability. Inside, routines protect us, yet they also limit love, freedom, and hope.

Certainty is an illusion, often fueled by pride and fear of change. True healing requires vulnerability, opening our mind, heart, and soul to connection.

Though stepping out may feel scary, small actions, like reaching out to others, engaging in our community, and practicing openness, allow us to reclaim life, experience love, and move toward wholeness beyond the walls we've built around ourselves.

DAY 348

Finding Hope in Recovery

Tammy sensed something was deeply wrong. Her mind was cloudy, and she felt weak and confused. Reaching out to her father, she acknowledged, "I am not bleeding, but something is terribly wrong."

Seeking professional help, she learned she had obsessive-compulsive and bipolar conditions. Her life could have followed despair . . . or Recovery. Turning points came through therapy, medication, and weekly women's support groups, where she felt love and belonging.

With guidance and treatment, Tammy found stability, hope, and the possibility of a normal life. She realized that storms pass, healing is possible, and love and support can transform even the darkest moments.

DAY 349

From Darkness to Light

Admitting that you have a mental health condition takes courage, but God meets us in our weakness. The darkness within us may feel heavy, like being trapped in a cave, yet God calls us into His healing light.

We have a choice: to remain hidden in fear or to step forward in faith. Recovery is not meant to be walked alone. When we open our hearts to God and to others, we discover love, trust, and new strength. In His light, we become the person He created us to be: whole, restored, and free.

DAY 350

Building Strength in the Journey

Daily reflections give us small but powerful steps toward healing. Each one is a reminder that we are serious about living differently, about becoming whole. Recovery does not always take away every symptom, yet it strengthens our spirit and gives us the tools to overcome them.

At times it may feel as if we are fighting against the current, going nowhere. But even then, God is building our inner strength. With patience and faith, new stamina grows within us. Slowly, the darkness loses its hold, our mood begins to lift, and hope lights the way forward.

DAY 351

Discovering a New Normal

Do you remember a time without sadness, fear, or anxiety? For some, these feelings have always seemed "normal." Yet when we begin to share our thoughts through journaling or with trusted people, healing begins. Slowly, we learn new ways of thinking and living.

The gift is a new normal, one filled with calm, clarity, and freedom. What once felt impossible becomes possible. Life begins to flow with purpose, connection, and hope. This gentle shift is evidence that our spirit is stronger than despair and that renewal is always within reach.

DAY 352

STEP #1

The Middle Path of Joy

Can desire for pleasure keep us trapped in suffering? Samantha believed alcohol was her pleasure, yet it only deepened her suffering. Fear told her that without drinking, depression and anxiety would consume her.

True change came when she learned to welcome suffering as a teacher rather than an enemy. In doing so, she discovered that joy is not found in pleasure but in living fully, embracing both suffering and beauty.

When we accept discomfort, we open our hearts to peace. The middle path leads us away from suffering and into freedom, beauty, and lasting joy.

DAY 353

The Beauty of Mindfulness

Mindfulness invites us to live fully in the present. It begins with three simple steps:

Stop: Slow down and notice what is happening within and around you.

Observe: Focus gently on one thing, such as your breath or the sensations in your body.

Return: When your thoughts drift to the past or future, bring yourself back with kindness to the present moment.

So often, we ignore the body's quiet messages or judge ourselves harshly. But when we stop, observe, and return, even difficult moments become easier to bear, and the joy of living becomes more available to us—anywhere, anytime.

DAY 354

Mindfulness and Self-Compassion

Mindfulness and self-compassion walk hand in hand. Through mindfulness, we learn not to cling to people, places, or things, and we allow painful thoughts and feelings to exist without being overwhelmed by them. When we over identify, we react intensely and lose ourselves in emotional storms.

Mindfulness, instead, sounds like: "I feel down, but I choose to meet my feelings with curiosity and openness." This gentle practice helps us pause, breathe, and cool off, so our natural desire for safety, joy, and health can rise. In this way, mindfulness becomes a steady part of Recovery and healing.

DAY 355

The Gift of Being Ourselves

When Fred was just seventeen, he was asked to counsel younger students on retreat. Unsure of how to lead, he sought advice from his teachers. The wisest response was simple: "Be yourself." That guidance shaped his life and allowed him to connect with others authentically.

Recovery is much the same. It invites us to walk with people who encourage, support, and breathe hope into us, not through authority but through compassion. Healing grows when we are free to be ourselves, supported by those who see our potential, and strengthened by the steps that lead us toward wholeness.

DAY 356

The Gift of Rest

Whether we are in Recovery or not, each of us has much to be grateful for: work, family, celebrations, and the daily responsibilities that bring meaning to life. Yet there are also seasons of waiting, preparation, and struggle when we feel weary or overwhelmed.

Sometimes rest is a sacred gift we give ourselves, a time to refuel our hearts, be grateful and quiet our minds for the journey ahead. In seasons of change, we are invited to welcome compassion, to pause, take a deep breath, and simply rest.

DAY 357

The Spirit of Recovery

Have you ever felt Recovery reach into the deepest places of your heart, revealing a joy you never imagined? Teresa, a stepmother to three young women, often feels this when they return home for a visit with their mother. Quietly, she whispers to herself, "I am so blessed to be part of their lives."

This love surprises her. It flows from a heart once closed by mental health struggles, now opened by Recovery. Learning to love herself taught her how to love others. Like a child discovering wonder, she embraces joy, kindness, and goodness. In that openness, the spirit of Recovery shines, reminding us love is always possible.

DAY 358

The Gift of Example

Anna has lived with bipolar disorder for over fifty years, yet her heart has never stopped actively working for her Recovery. Each day she follows her plan, gives thanks, and prays for others on their journey.

Her quiet dedication reminds us that healing is possible. Recovery is unique for each of us, through prayer, rest, care, and connection. When we align ourselves with those like Anna, their wisdom and example feed our hearts. Showing up, listening, and learning allows the miracle of well-being to touch our lives, guiding us gently toward hope, love, and wholeness.

DAY 359

STEP #10

The Gentle Call

A Higher Power's call is not always found on mountaintops or in retreats; it meets us in the ordinary rhythms of life. Recovery reminds us we are met right where we are, in quiet moments, in daily work, in the simple stirring of the heart.

Several years ago, I felt such a nudge and began a peer support group. No fireworks, only a whisper that has kept me steady on the path of healing. Recovery's call is like this: tender, persistent, inviting us to live, to love, and to follow whenever the heart quietly says, *"Come."*

DAY 360

The Gift of Rest

Life offers us much to be grateful for: work, family, celebrations, and daily routines. Yet there are seasons of waiting and preparation that can feel overwhelming and exhausting. In these times, it is wise to rest, let go of our struggles and listen for the voice of God to help direct our choices.

Rest becomes a sacred pause, not an escape from challenges but a renewal for the journey ahead. When we admit our need for rest, burdens lighten, and hope is restored. Surrounded by love, especially within our Recovery community, we rediscover childlike joy and strength for the next step forward.

DAY 361

Love Unveiled

Recovery has a way of reaching into hidden places of the soul, uncovering joy we never imagined. Tom, a stepfather, discovers this blessing when his daughters return home from a visit with their father. In a quiet moment, his heart whispers, *I am so blessed.*

This love, once unseen, awakens through the tender work of Recovery, teaching us first to love ourselves, so we may truly love others. It is a childlike gift, opening us to kindness, wonder, and grace. In these moments, we touch the spirit of healing, where love itself becomes both the path and the promise.

DAY 362

Under Our Roof

Step 7 reminds us: "We accept God's unconditional love and compassion into our lives."

This love enters our lives much like an unexpected guest, seeing us as we truly are, dust and all. There is no hiding, no need to clean up first.

Though we may feel unworthy, God meets us in our homes, workplaces, and schools with mercy, compassion, and healing. Recovery is not only for ourselves but also for those we love. In welcoming love under our roof, we discover hope, wholeness, and the quiet presence of God.

DAY 363

The Gentle Voice of a Wise Mind

In Recovery, a wise mind comes as a quiet guide, balancing thought and feeling, reason and emotion. It does not silence our hearts nor dismiss our minds. Instead, it weaves them together, like soft notes forming a healing song.

When we are faced with suffering, our wise mind reminds us to pause, to breathe, to see clearly. In its harmony we find peace, strength, and the courage to continue.

Today, listen for its gentle voice within, trusting it to lead you with compassion into the next step of your journey.

DAY 364

Acting from Love

Recovery teaches mercy, generosity, forgiveness, and love, guiding us to act from the heart, not for recognition.

Like attending a childhood basketball practice, some actions are simply what we are called to do. In Recovery, our faith and beliefs shape our actions, supporting others and honoring our Higher Power. When we act from love for our peers, family, and community, our efforts naturally align with what is good. Mindfulness helps us notice these moments, allowing our hearts to follow the vision we are meant to live.

DAY 365

The Table of Community

Humanity calls us to recognize what we share. At a banquet or wedding, we come together through connection, young and old, rich and poor, able-bodied and disabled. We celebrate diversity yet unite in common longing for meaning and belonging.

The table of Recovery is a great equalizer, inviting all to be fed without regard for circumstance. Gathered in community (whether at family, church, sports, or support groups), we practice authentic living. Here, love, compassion, and presence transform us. Through these shared moments, we grow, heal, and step closer to the best version of ourselves, guided by God's quiet wisdom.

A WELCOME TO RECOVERY

Recovery is a journey of hope, courage, and love. It invites us to look honestly at ourselves, seek guidance from God, and connect with others who support our growth. These steps are not meant to be perfected. Instead, they help us learn, heal, and open our hearts to God's love.

The beliefs that guide us through Recovery help us grow spiritually, emotionally, and mentally. The term *God* can also mean *Higher Power*. These steps work for anyone—whether we call on the Christian God or another spiritual Higher Power.

TWELVE STEPS OF RECOVERY

1 We believe that Recovery is possible. With courage and hope, we commit to overcoming the internal and external barriers that stand in our way.

2 We believe that a loving God will restore us spiritually, emotionally, and mentally.

3 We decrease our human desires in order to increase the voice of God in our lives.

4 We make a Recovery plan after an honest reflection of our behavior.

5 We share our Recovery plan with God and other people that support us.

6 We surrender to God our suffering, anger, resentments, and other emotions blocking our Recovery.

7 We accept God's unconditional love and compassion into our lives.

8 We connect with peers in Recovery and invite their presences into our lives.

9   We are imperfect human beings. Make amends to a person when necessary, then release shame, guilt, and other emotions getting in the way of our growth.

10   We continue to review our recovery plan and revise it when necessary.

11   We realize Recovery is not just an intention but also action. Through prayer, reflection, and mindfulness, we seek guidance from God and people in our support network.

12   We are having a spiritual awakening as a result of our Recovery. We are learning to love ourselves and others. We practice these steps in all of our affairs.

Adapted from
"The Twelve Steps," Alcoholics Anonymous,
https://www.aa.org/the-twelve-steps.

ACKNOWLEDGMENTS

I want to thank my wife for her loving moral and financial support during the last four years of writing this daily devotional. You are my soul mate, my partner in every way, and together we make a wonderful team.

Special recognition goes to **Azul Terronez** from Authors Who Lead. After reviewing my first manuscript, he challenged me to reduce it from 90,000 words to 36,000. At first, I was anxious. I didn't want to lose the heart of the message. But I placed my faith in his wisdom. Now, I see how right he was. The final version is clear, powerful, and the message shines through beautifully.

Each week, I met with **The Leaders Circle**, part of the Authors Who Lead Community. This amazing group of authors gives me a safe space to be open, honest, and to grow both as a writer and as a person. My heartfelt thanks to **Steve Vannoy**, **Sybil Hall**, **Abby Medcalf**, **Heather Lee Dyer (Perrault)**, **Mari Ruddy**, and **Tobi Johnson** for their encouragement and friendship.

I also owe deep gratitude to the **mental health and substance misuse support groups** I attend weekly. You are the heartbeat of this devotional. Together, we laugh, cry, and share our struggles with honesty and hope. You have inspired me more than words can express, and I feel eternally blessed to walk beside you.

Finally, I want to thank **Amanda Toynbee** from Authors Who Lead for coordinating this entire project from the moment I sent my manuscript until publication day. Thank you for your guidance, patience, and kindness every step of the way. You helped make this dream a reality.

ABOUT THE AUTHOR

L. J. Winter grew up in a small farming community in northeastern Wisconsin. Basketball became his refuge while facing a mother with bipolar disorder, a father struggling to hold the family together, and his own mental health challenges.

By middle school, he experienced depression and anxiety. In his late twenties, he sought help from a therapist and psychiatrist and was formally diagnosed. His therapist encouraged him to keep a daily journal to better understand his mind and track his Recovery.

For thirty years, he journaled off and on. In his late forties, a personality test suggested he try writing. After retiring from a thirty-year social work career at age fifty-five, he became an author. Encouraged by his father, he wrote *SuperHuman Being*, sharing their family's experiences with mental health, trauma, and substance misuse.

Today, L. J. is a Certified Peer Specialist with lived experience in mental health, addiction, and trauma. He facilitates a weekly virtual Peer Support Group and serves on a local Mental Health Task Force. Through his work, he offers hope, guidance, and connection, showing that Recovery is possible and that each person's life is valuable.

You can purchase my first book on Amazon or it is also
available on my website: superhumanbeing.net

I would appreciate your feedback on what days helped you
most and what you would like to see in future books.

Contact me at: ljw@superhumanbeing.net

If you enjoyed this book and found it helpful,
please leave a review on Amazon.

Visit me at

SUPERHUMANBEING.NET

where you can sign up to receive my daily blog full of inspiration
and actions you can take to manage your mental wellness.

Thank you!